ENRICHMENT ACTIVITIES
for Gifted Students

ENRICHMENT ACTIVITIES
for Gifted Students

Extracurricular Academic Activities
for Gifted Education

Todd Stanley

Routledge
Taylor & Francis Group

NEW YORK AND LONDON

First published in 2021 by Prufrock Press Inc.

Published 2021 by Routledge
605 Third Avenue, New York, NY 10017
2 Park Square, Milton Park, Abingdon, Oxon OX14 4RN

Routledge is an imprint of the Taylor & Francis Group, an informa business

Library of Congress Control Number: 2020949073

ISBN 13: 978-1-0321-4224-1 (hbk)
ISBN 13: 978-1-6463-2083-7 (pbk)

DOI: 10.4324/9781003234982

Table of Contents

Introduction

During the school day in the United States, the focus is typically on academics. Bells ring, students move from classroom to classroom, and the main goal of each day is for students to learn intellectual skills and content. When the final bell rings, however, most schools shift their focus from academics to sports. For example, nearly 60% of 12th-grade students are involved in athletics (Veliz et al., 2019), with there often being 15 different sports to choose from, scheduled throughout the fall, winter, and spring seasons. There is no disputing that sports teach skills, whether they be related to the sport itself, such as throwing, catching, running, or hitting, or whether they are extremely valuable 21st-century skills, such as collaboration, leadership, adaptation, communication, and initiative. In fact, one could argue that athletics teaches these skills more transparently and better than does the classroom.

Depending on the school system you are in, however, the past few decades have been building to a tipping point. Although previously sports were perhaps just a way to get some exercise and/ or physical activity, they have now become the main focus of many

DOI: 10.4324/9781003234982-1

students and members of the district. Although a district would most likely never admit to this, the sports focus is exhibited every day in the fact that there are trophy cases at the front of the school lauding the many athletic accomplishments, the morning announcements are rife with sports updates rather than academic information, and on Friday nights during the fall, the football stadiums are packed with students and community members. Meanwhile, the only people coming to the spelling bee or the quiz bowl are the parents of the participants. Communities may spend millions of dollars on stadiums and turf that could be put toward more academic ventures, and there are schools that hire teachers based on their coaching abilities rather than how they grow students academically in the classroom.

This focus on sports is further accentuated at the college level, where the National Collegiate Athletic Association (NCAA) brings in more than $1 billion in annual revenue and has become the minor leagues for many professional sports. College athletes collectively, on average, are awarded $2.9 billion in scholarship money (Berkowitz, 2018). College sports have become a big business, and some students and families count on athletics taking them further than academics would. This trickles down to the high school and even junior high levels, where children have started training year-round in a single sport and where the summer baseball schedule of 10 games over the course of 3 months has become 160 games on a travel team.

These realizations led me to a ground-breaking thought: What if educators at all levels started to pay attention to academic extracurricular activities (AECAs) as much as they do athletic ones? I am not suggesting schools jettison sports from schools like many Eastern Hemisphere school systems do, where sports are run as a club separate from the schools. I am just asking for equal treatment—that the funds schools use for sports are the same afforded to AECAs, that there is room in the trophy cases and on the announcements for the accomplishments of these academic competitors, and that the school pep rallies and media give as much attention to these activities as they do athletics. What if schools were used to recognize and support academic excellence, whether it is in the classroom or outside of it?

In the October 2019 issue of *Gifted Children Quarterly*, Jonathan Wai and Jeff Allen wrote about what boosts the talent development of gifted students in secondary education. They looked at 21 years of data to determine effective ways to help gifted students develop their talents. They found that the usual suspects, such as STEM courses, Advanced Placement (AP) courses, and College Credit Plus (CCP) or postsecondary classes, are proven to increase a student's educational growth.

Wai and Allen (2019) also looked at extracurricular activities and the effect they had on academic growth. The results were mixed. Activities such as community service, debate, performing arts, or cultural clubs were found to have positive effects on students' academic growth. Nonacademic clubs such as social clubs, radio/TV, or sports were shown to have a negative impact on student achievement growth.

Wai and Allen (2019) concluded that "how academically talented students allocate their time is of potential importance" (p. 16). In other words, some extracurricular activities will develop talent better than others. Students just need to choose the right ones. This begs the question: What are worthwhile extracurricular activities that students can participate in to develop their academic talents? That is the purpose of this book—to help you to find academic extracurricular activities that will boost the intellectual abilities of your gifted students, and any student, for that matter.

How to Use This Book

Here is the way this book is set up. I have broken down the academic extracurricular activities (AECAs) by subject area, and for each of these areas, I have five examples detailed with the 5 W's (and 1 H).

What Is This Activity?

Each example incudes a brief overview, describing the general idea of what someone running it should expect as well as what students will be doing.

Who Can Be Involved?

This is simply the grade and age levels this particular AECA is suited for. Some nationally known programs are for a certain grade range, such as MATHCOUNTS, which is for grades 6–8, or DECA, which is for high school and college students. This does not preclude you from having students participate in these activities; it just might mean they will not compete against other teams in an official capacity. For instance, Future City Competition is aimed at students in sixth, seventh, and eighth grade, but this did not stop me from having a scaled version of it for third and fourth graders. Students still used *Sim City* to develop their cities, but instead of participating in the Future City Competition, they just presented their cities to an outside, authentic audience that I arranged.

Where Does This Activity Take Place?

This means where the competition takes place if it is a national program. For instance, Destination Imagination first starts with regional tournaments held all over the state. The size of the state affects how many regional tournaments there are. For example, Oregon has three different regions, while Texas has 17. The higher performing teams are then invited to compete at the state tournament, which takes place a few weeks later and is usually in a single location. The highest performers at the state tournaments compete at the global competition, which brings together more than 1,000 teams from all over the world, usually at the end of May, in a single city determined by Destination Imagination International.

When Does This Activity Occur?

Each example includes when the event takes place. The AECA could be a recurring event taking place once a week, such as a Dungeons and Dragons club, or one that culminates in a single event, such as World Maths Day. If you are participating in a national program, the event date is likely already determined for you. If you are conducting a chess club and the culminating event is a districtwide chess tournament, you could decide the event date for yourself. Some AECAs involve a yearlong process during which the participating students work on the task over the course of the year only to show what they have accomplished toward the end of the year. Others do not have a year-end event but rather a window in which to compete. For instance, in the WordMasters Challenge, the advisor can schedule when they would like to give the three tests students take. The official organization simply provides you, as the advisor, with deadlines for submitting student scores.

Why Should Students Participate?

Ultimately, you want your students to benefit by participating in an AECA. This section lays out the benefits for students participating in the example activity and how it boosts their academic skills, especially 21st-century ones. Public speaking, critical thinking, problem solving, creativity, initiative, information literacy, and collaboration are just some of the valuable, real-world skills students will be able to apply to their future.

How Do You Run This Activity?

Most of the AECAs detailed in this book are ones that I have run or been involved with for several years, a few for more than a decade. In this section, for each example, I will lay out how I ran the program. For those programs I have not been involved with, I have interviewed educators who have coached these activities and asked them about the best ways to set up and run the particular AECA. In most cases there is not just one way to run an AECA, but I will attempt to show a blueprint for what running each might look like.

Many of the AECA examples are associated with national or statewide organizers. This way, you, as the advisor, do not have to start from scratch. In many cases, there is already a curriculum in place and/or a structure to work from. I also include in each chapter a fifth AECA that can be homegrown by the advisor and students.

Time to Get Started

One thing I have learned over my years in education is that for any of these academic extracurricular activities to work, you need to have an advocate willing to put in the time and endure the headaches that come with such a role. Hopefully by the time you have finished this book, you will have developed an interest in championing for one or more of these AECAs and will have the confidence to move forward in guiding students to success within them. Success does not mean winning the state championship or receiving national recognition, although those things are certainly icing on the cake. Success means that the students will have gotten something out of the AECA to put in their toolbox of skills that will greatly help them be successful in life. At the end of the day, that is what we, as educators, are trying to accomplish with our students. We want the learning to transcend the lessons of the classroom and provide children with the means to make their dreams and aspirations come true.

CHAPTER 1

The Benefits of Academic Extracurricular Activities

Why should students participate in an academic extracurricular activity? Shouldn't what happens during the school day be enough for their education? Don't students need a break from using their brains, some time to be themselves, and some time to relax? This is absolutely the case. Students should be out doing what they are passionate about, whether it be playing video games, rehearsing with their rock band, skateboarding, or participating in a sport. But here is the thing: Many students are passionate about learning. I know—*microphone drop, mind blown*—but it's true. Some kids want to go more in depth than their classes and teachers provide and explore subjects in more authentic settings.

Educational reasons aside, academic extracurricular activities are fun. What could be more fun than designing a robot that can shoot a basketball 15 feet . . . or submitting for publication your very own short story that you have written? Imagine the rush when the equation you have been studying and tweaking suddenly becomes clear while competing in the National Number Knockout competition. Many academic extracurricular activities are also based on

DOI: 10.4324/9781003234982-2

competition, and this competition can be fun and can raise the level of challenge and enjoyment for all involved.

In addition, students get the opportunity to show school spirit by representing their school at the competition. One cannot say that "all gifted students who participate in AECAs lack athleticism," but imagine you are a student who does not care for athletics. What can you do to support your school? What avenue do you have to show school pride? How can you get recognition for skills you have that are not based on athleticism? AECAs give students an outlet to be a bigger part of the school culture and to feel as though they are contributing to the overall reputation of the school.

Fun and pride aside, there are lots of benefits that participating in AECAs provide a student. The most obvious is that AECAs teach a specific skill in a specific subject area depending on the activity in which students are participating. Students might learn about complex math by participating in the Continental Mathematics League, become more familiar with language through the International Linguistics Olympiad, or learn how economics work in the real world through DECA.

21st-Century Skills

I would argue that most AECAs teach students skills that transcend content. Most teach valuable 21st-century skills, learning that may not be happening in the classroom as much as it should. Why are 21st-century skills so important? Because a person is not prevented from being successful in later life if they don't know the answer to a question in the National Geographic Bee, or if they miss a few problems on World Maths Day, or if their Genius Hour project utterly fails. Twenty-first-century skills, however, are extremely important for a student's future. If the student never learns how to effectively communicate orally, they might have difficulty with relationships. If they are poor at collaboration, it could affect their ability to do their job effectively or be viewed as a valuable team member. If they do not show much initiative, they may not earn a future promotion. The student will watch as others who show initiative pass them by. Learning 21st-century skills is important because they are life skills or, as Tony Wagner (2014) referred to them in his book *The Global Achievement Gap*, survival skills. He maintained that every student should leave the classroom with seven particular skills if they are going to compete in the global marketplace, all of which can be learned by participating in AECAs:

1. **Critical Thinking and Problem Solving:** These should be happening on a daily basis in the classroom, but many would be surprised that they

are not. One might think that if you are in a math class working on an equation, you are problem solving, but in actuality you are solving a problem. There is a distinct difference: Problem solving is when something unexpected or challenging is presented and you must try to come up with a creative or innovative solution out of many possibilities. This describes many AECAs, in that they involve students being presented with a dilemma, world issue, challenge, or question, and students must think critically to determine an effective and creative way to solve it. You could have 50 teams using the same prompt, and all 50 of them might come up with a different solution.

2. **Collaboration Across Networks and Leading by Influence:** Can a student work well with others in order to produce something as a group that is better than what could have been done by any one individual? Many AECAs teach collaboration by putting students into a team and requiring them to move the ship as a whole rather than individually paddling. Like a baseball team, no one player is the team. Everyone must do their part in order to succeed. This is a very important skill to possess not only in the workforce, but also in everyday life. No matter where your life takes you, you will encounter some sort of collaboration, whether it be family, friends, or hobbies. In the workplace it is really vital because no company is one person. Companies are made up of multiple employees, all working together for the benefit of the whole. Those companies that are well known for their collaborations are often the most successful. Thus, successful companies want to hire good collaborators.

3. **Agility and Adaptability:** When things don't go their way or as they expected, how good are your students at pivoting and moving forward? Being able to adapt makes students valuable to potential employers. Whether you are a doctor who has to change your course of treatment if a patient does not improve as expected, or a waiter who has a patron who has changed their mind about their meal, things change midcourse and you have to be prepared for it. As a teacher, how many times has something not gone according to plan and you have had to adapt the lesson for a better learning experience? If you're like me, this is an everyday occurrence. Those who are not able to adapt often produce inferior work or simply get left behind. We don't want our students to get left behind. AECAs usually start with an initial problem for students to study, and additional layers of complexity come into play as students progress. Students learn to adapt, as their performance at the competition will look very different then they imagined it would be. Adaptation teaches students grit and perseverance because when things do not go

as planned, the team comes up with plan B, C, D, or however many it takes. Students unable to adapt may have trouble when they struggle with real-world problems in the future.

4. **Initiative and Entrepreneurialism:** Initiative is one's ability to take on a task, not because someone has told them or required them to do it, but because it is something they have determined needs to be done or they see the benefit in doing so. Many students involved in AECAs show tremendous initiative just by being there. After all, what they are doing is typically not a requirement; they are choosing to be involved and participate. They give up before- and/or afterschool time. They perform on evenings or weekends. They sacrifice time that they might have spent doing some other leisure activity. Showing initiative relies on the choice of the individual, and students are choosing to be involved. If your AECA is set up well, students will have plenty of opportunity to show initiative. After all, just like sports, it is those who practice the hardest and put in the extra work not required of them who find the most success. There usually is no grade for an AECA, so students need to decide for themselves how far they want to take their work.

5. **Effective Oral and Written Communication:** Being able to communicate orally effectively is a skill not everyone possesses. In fact, it is estimated that as many as 75% of the population has anxiety about speaking in public (Black, 2019). Imagine how valuable you would be to a future employer if you are part of the 25% that isn't. And how do you get better at oral communication? Just like a sport, the more you do it, the more comfortable you become. Putting students in situations where they not only have to perform in spoken form, but also must do so to an authentic audience that brings a real-world application, is a great way to help them learn this skill. Many, but not all, of the AECAs have a performance aspect to them in which students are either presenting to a panel of judges, giving an actual performance to an audience, or having to talk to someone in an authentic situation. This experience will pay off, as students become not only proficient at oral communication, but also able to thrive at it. If there is not an oral aspect, there is usually a written one in which students must show what they have learned. Either way, students must clearly communicate the merits of their solution. Other than collaboration, I feel that communication is one of the most important skills I can teach my students, as not a lot of other teachers focus on this type of performance assessment.

6. **Accessing and Analyzing Information:** This is one's ability to find information as well as determine whether it is reliable. This is a valuable skill to possess because students will spend a lot of their adult lives try-

ing to find information that is going to help them, whether it be determining what sort of house they can purchase, researching a place to take the family for vacation, looking for instructions for changing a faucet head, or just trying to decide which movie to see. Students will also use this skill in their occupation. Doctors have to consider new research and how this might affect the way they practice medicine. Stockbrokers have to study past performances of certain stocks and then make a prediction of how one will perform in the future, deciding whether their client should purchase it or not. Teachers have to find information and strategies for educating their students and make sure what is being provided is accurate. This skill harkens to one of my educational philosophies: Rather than teaching my students facts, I want to teach them where they can find facts for themselves.

7. **Curiosity and Imagination:** Educators do not let students use curiosity and imagination in schools as much as we should. Children are innately curious about the world, especially when they are younger and there is still so much that is unknown. By the time they get to high school, though, a lot of students' curiosity and imagination has been tamped down by content and standards. How often are students allowed to explore their curiosity in a math class? How many times has a student used their imagination in social studies? Out in the business world, it is this curiosity and imagination that lead to new and better products. Where would Apple be without imagination? Where would Elon Musk be without curiosity? Without curiosity and imagination, there wouldn't be any innovations. Things would merely stay the same. Think about a company that is interviewing two candidates. One produces by-the-book products, and another has an innovative imagination, never doing the same thing twice. Which one do you think will be hired?

Not all of the AECAs presented in this book expose students to and teach students all seven of the survival skills, but there are many that do. Let's take Business Professionals of America's Website Design Team competition as an example. In a nutshell, a team must create an effective website based on a prompt. The team must not only develop the website, but also present the website to a panel of experts. The following list breaks down how students will practice all of the survival skills in this competition:

1. **Critical Thinking and Problem Solving:** The team must determine the design and layout of the website, create graphics that are visually attractive to draw people in, and then code the site so that it works effectively. This all involves critical thinking and problem solving. There is no one correct answer for this task. Instead, there are numerous possibilities,

and students must analyze and then figure out how to make it all actually work. It requires everyone doing their role and doing it well.

2. **Collaboration Across Networks and Leading by Influence:** This competition is a team effort, so being able to collaborate and lead effectively is tantamount. Without effective teamwork, something may get overlooked, leaving the product incomplete or riddled with errors.

3. **Agility and Adaptability:** The team must adapt to the prompt and make adjustments throughout the course of the competition. The students might make it to the state-level competition and receive valuable feedback on how they can make their site better for the national competition, leading them to improve their product.

4. **Initiative and Entrepreneurialism:** This is a project that cannot be completed just during dedicated AECA time. The students have to take it upon themselves to put in extra work to make sure that their product is of the highest quality without the advisor having to check in constantly.

5. **Effective Oral and Written Communication:** The team must not only have effective written communication on their website so that those navigating it know to use it, but also orally present their website and justify their choices to a panel of experts.

6. **Accessing and Analyzing Information:** The team must conduct research that will be put onto the website in order to inform consumers.

7. **Curiosity and Imagination:** A boring ol' website is not going to cut it. The students must use their imaginations to create something that stands out from the thousands of other participants.

As noted, not all AECAs allow students to practice all of these skills. Some AECAs are individual competitions so collaboration might not come into play. Others may not have an oral aspect to the product. Some do not require any research in order to compete, so analyzing and accessing information may not be a significant factor. But all of the AECAs shared in this book teach many of these 21st-century skills.

Something Extra to Think About

If you need more evidence to convince you of the value of AECAs, consider the 2018 Future of Jobs Report (World Economic Forum, 2018). The top 10 job skills predicted for 2022 are:

1. analytical thinking and innovation;

2. active learning and learning strategies;
3. creativity, originality, and initiative;
4. technology design and programming;
5. critical thinking and analysis;
6. complex problem solving;
7. leadership and social influence;
8. emotional intelligence;
9. reasoning, problem solving, and ideation; and
10. systems analysis and evaluation.

Many of these align with the 21st-century skills discussed previously. The only one that does not match up with one of the survival skills is emotional intelligence. Emotional intelligence is defined by Peter Salovey and John Mayer as:

> the ability to monitor one's own and other people's emotions, to discriminate between different emotions and label them appropriately, and to use emotional information to guide thinking and behavior. (as cited in Cherry, 2019, sec. 11, para. 6)

The key is the last part of the definition—the part that says people should use emotional information to guide thinking and behavior. If a student has all of the other 21st-century survival skills, they certainly use emotional information to guide thinking and behavior. This is what allows them to be successful in collaboration, drives their ability to show initiative, and provides them with the fortitude to adapt to challenging situations. In addition, emotional intelligence is used quite a bit in critical thinking, especially when it is authentic and can be applied to the real world, having to consider other people's perspectives as well. If we are able to teach students how to use these survival skills effectively, they will be attractive to employers and have a tool kit of skills that can be applied to their lives, rather than merely learning content that will not.

CHAPTER **2**

English Language Arts

I start with English language arts (ELA) because more than any other subject area, it permeates through all of the others. Students will do a lot of reading in social studies, a lot of writing in science, and a lot of comprehension in math. Many ELA skills are ones that students will end up using the rest of their lives, no matter what profession they end up in. There may be a lot of school-specific math skills, social studies content, and science concepts that will fall by the wayside once leaving school, but ELA skills are something everyone uses every day.

With that in mind, the more we can do to strengthen these ELA skills or, more importantly, show students how to use them in an authentic situation, the better prepared they are going to be when they run across a situation that requires these skills in their real lives. The five AECAs in this chapter cover a lot of different skills, from writing, to reading, to vocabulary, to linguistics.

DOI: 10.4324/9781003234982-3

Scholastic Art & Writing Awards

What Is This Activity?

The Scholastic Art & Writing Awards (https://www.artandwriting.org), presented by the Alliance for Young Artists & Writers, are part of a writing contest that has been around since 1923 and accepts submissions from public, private, and home schools. The Alliance's mission is to:

> identify students with exceptional artistic and literary talent and present their remarkable work to the world through the Scholastic Art & Writing Awards. The Awards give students opportunities for recognition, exhibition, publication, and scholarships. Students across America submitted nearly 320,000 original works [in 2020] in 29 different categories of art and writing. (Scholastic Art & Writing Awards, n.d.-a, para. 1)

Who Can Be Involved?

The Scholastic Art & Writing Awards take entries from students grades 7–12, or ages 13 and up. There are 11 categories of writing (see https://www.artandwriting.org/awards/how-to-enter/categories):

1. Critical essay
2. Dramatic script
3. Flash fiction
4. Humor
5. Journalism
6. Novel writing
7. Personal essay & memoir
8. Poetry
9. Science fiction & fantasy
10. Short story
11. Writing portfolio

(*Note.* There are also 18 art categories for students who are artistically inclined.)

The 11th writing category is for graduating seniors and tasks them with writing a portfolio that acts as a capstone for their journey in writing. Every category has specific parameters and expectations. For example, here are the requirements for the personal essay and memoir category:

Personal Essay & Memoir:
A non-fiction work based on opinion, experience, and/or emotion that explores a topic or event of importance to the author.

Limits:
500–3,000 words

The organization provides examples of past work that can be used as exemplars or for students to get a sense of the requirements for a piece in each category. These can be accessed at https://www.artandwriting.org/gallery.

Where Does This Activity Take Place?

Unlike some academic competitions, this is not one in which students gather to compete directly with one another. Instead, students individually register on the website for the Scholastic Art & Writing Awards and then submit their entry electronically. They also send a hard copy to their local affiliate, along with their payment, usually around $7 an entry. If their piece of writing is recognized, students can attend their affiliate ceremony, which honors those who had outstanding pieces of writing. In order to find out where your affiliate is located, visit https://www.artandwriting.org/regions.

When Does This Activity Occur?

The writing submissions are processed and judged first at the regional level by affiliate partner organizations that set their own deadlines, but most are due mid-December. Winners are announced at the end of January. Students who receive Gold Key, Silver Key, and Honorable Mention awards are celebrated in local exhibitions and ceremonies across the country. If a student receives a Gold Key delineation, they are considered for advancement to the national level, where work is evaluated by some of the foremost leaders in the visual and literary arts, including literary agents, editors, professors, screenwriters, award-winning poets, and executives from nonprofit organizations. If by chance a student writer is recognized as being a Gold Key designee by the national awards committee, they are invited to attend a ceremony in early June in New York City.

Why Should Students Participate?

Although there are general requirements for entries, including word count and genre, students are allowed to express themselves freely through the written word. As the website states:

> writers are free to explore any and all topics. There are no predefined prompts and no work is ever disqualified from the Scholastic Awards because of the nature of its content. (Scholastic Art & Writing Awards, n.d.-b, para. 10)

Students are encouraged to think outside of the box, which is evidenced by the judging criteria:

- **Originality:** Work that breaks from convention, blurs the boundaries between genres, and challenges notions of how a particular concept or emotion can be expressed.
- **Technical Skill:** Work that uses technique to advance an original perspective or a personal vision or voice, and shows skills being utilized to create something unique, powerful, and innovative.
- **Emergence of a Personal Vision or Voice:** Work with an authentic and unique point of view and style. (Scholastic Art & Writing Awards, n.d.-b, para. 11–13)

Students not only learn the craft of written communication, but also how to be creative and express their voice. This is especially important for gifted students identified in creative thinking because there is not a lot of service in this area at the middle and high school levels. This AECA allows them to use their ability to think creatively in order to construct their story and describe its action.

Writing can be a very cruel profession, so providing students with a safe place where they can express themselves and pursue a piece of writing they are passionate about can help students to see how writing is used in the real world. Writing is an authentic skill students can build.

How Do You Run This Activity?

Most writing in the classroom is of an academic nature. There is not a lot of time spent in typical ELA courses on freely writing fiction or poetry. With that in mind, I would run this as a before-school or afterschool activity. Unlike some clubs that would need to meet every week, most of the work can be done independently by the students, developing their initiative. Your role as the advisor would be to make sure they are aware of deadlines and that they have properly registered and submitted their entry.

Because most of the entries are due in mid-December, you will want to provide students with enough time to be able to develop their written work, including the revising and editing process. With this in mind, you should start early in the school year and provide a space where students can workshop their pieces in order to receive feedback and advice from fellow students.

You might have monthly meetings to check in with students or to teach skills, such as revising and editing, basic story structure, grammar rules, or appropriate vocabulary, but you could communicate more often through email, group chats, and Google Docs. Provide students with deadlines throughout the process. When is their first draft due? When is the second? You do not want to simply give them the deadline for the final draft because then some students with poor time management will wait until then to try to write their story, usually with inferior results.

You will have to decide how the entries are going to be paid for. Are students and families going to pay the $7 themselves, or is the school going to support the entries? If the latter, make sure you give your district enough time to process the payments. There is an option for students who qualify for free and/or reduced lunch. They simply have to fill out a form from the award website and have a parent sign it.

WordMasters Challenge

What Is This Activity?

Many language arts competitions focus on grammar, punctuation, spelling, or other language mechanics. The WordMasters Challenge (https://www.word masterschallenge.com) is designed to help students think analytically and metaphorically, as well as learn some vocabulary along the way, through analogies. As the website states:

> Excellence in the competition will require both a mastery of the meanings of the vocabulary words (of a difficulty appropriate to each grade level) and thoughtful reasoning about the relationships between these words and more familiar language used in the competition's analogies. (WordMasters Challenge, n.d., para. 5)

Students are given a list of vocabulary terms, usually consisting of 25 words. Students are tasked with not only determining the definition, or in many cases definitions, of each word, but also understanding the words enough that they can associate them with other words in an analogy. For instance, if a given word is *virus*, a student would have to look up this word and determine that it means a submicroscopic agent that affects living organisms, or in more user-friendly words, something that causes sickness. There could even be an alternate definition: a program that infects computers or causes them to not work properly. This will eventually be presented in an analogy in which students have to determine the relationship between two words. For example, if the analogy is, Virus : Sick, the relationship here is that viruses *cause* sickness. You would have to find a similar relationship amongst the choices provided:

- Fly : Kite
- Nice : Pleasant
- Carelessness : Errors
- Turtle : Slow

In this example, the student has to determine the relationships between the words and match it with the original analogy. Of these choices, only Carelessness *causes* Errors, so that would be the correct answer.

Three times during the course of the school year, students are given a test with 20 questions that includes analogies that use the words they have been studying from the list. Prior to each of these tests, they will receive three word lists that they can study.

Who Can Be Involved?

WordMasters is open to grades 3–8. Each grade level is given a different list. The word lists are designed to be more challenging with each advancing grade. There is also a blue and gold list within a grade level, the gold list being the more challenging of them. This list would be ideal for gifted students or those who are advanced in ELA. WordMasters costs around $100 per team that you register. Teams are determined by grade level and whether each student is taking the blue or the gold test. In other words, if you have some students in the seventh grade taking the blue test, but you are having the honors class take the gold test, that would be two separate teams.

The teams can be as large as you want them to be (you could have the entire fourth grade taking the test). Only the top 10 scores get reported to WordMasters, and these scores are used to calculate the team score.

Where Does This Activity Take Place?

WordMasters takes place in your local classroom or school. A teacher/advisor would need to supervise the test to make sure results are legitimate. After students take the test, they are graded by the teacher/advisor. The top 10 scores are submitted by this person on the WordMasters website, which determines the team score. WordMasters then creates a report that shows how your students scored compared to others in their grade and division.

After the three tests, the statistics are all compiled, and the top 100 teams and top 200 individual students are recognized by WordMasters. The teacher/advisor is provided with 10 certificates for the top 10 scorers for the year, as well as a champion medal for your top scorer. If you want additional medals or certificates, they can be ordered at https://app.wordmasterschallenge.com/storefront/c/merchandise. Your class or school can decide if you want to recognize these students at a ceremony, at a pep rally, on the school announcements, or by the school board. It is important that these students are honored for their academic achievements.

When Does This Activity Occur?

The school or club advisor holds three analogy meets throughout the year, one by December, one by February, and the final one by April. The general schedule looks like Figure 1. As you can see, the schedule starts in October and goes all of the way through the end of school in May. You will also notice there are windows in which to take the tests. Each window is usually a couple of weeks long, and the teacher/advisor can decide for themselves when it is best to have the students take the test. The teacher/advisor just needs to be sure they get the tests graded and submitted online to WordMasters by the reporting deadline.

Why Should Students Participate?

This competition develops several skills. First, it increases the vocabulary of students as they learn about words they are unfamiliar with and how to use them properly. Anything that can extend the vocabulary of a student is going to benefit both their written and spoken responses. Unlike a spelling bee, which involves simple recall, students participating in WordMasters are also developing critical thinking skills, which is the best way to challenge gifted students. Knowledge is not enough; you must provide a place for gifted students to take this knowledge, analyze and evaluate it, and create a new idea. It is not enough to simply know a word—this is why WordMasters works for well for this group.

FIGURE 1
Sample WordMasters Schedule

Challenge Meet #1	
Word Lists Available Online	October 1
Tests Available Online	Early November
Tests Administered	Mid-November
Score Reporting Deadline	Early December
Results Available	Late December
Challenge Meet #2	
Word Lists Available Online	Early December
Tests Available Online	Late January
Tests Administered	Early–Mid-February
Score Reporting Deadline	Late February
Results Available	Mid-March
Challenge Meet #3	
Word Lists Available Online	Early March
Tests Available Online	Early April
Tests Administered	Mid–Late April
Score Reporting Deadline	Early May
Results Available	Early–Mid-May
Cumulative Champions Announced	Early–Mid-May

Note. Adapted from "WordMasters Challenge Schedule," by WordMasters Challenge, 2020, https://www.wordmasterschallenge.com/challenge-schedule.

Students must analyze the relationship between the two words, and then associate them with two other words with the same relationship. This is a deeper level of thinking than a simple recall of facts. Students have to put their brains to work. It also creates good study habits, which some gifted students can take for granted, depending on their natural abilities. Students are charged with defining the words and then learning them, not just for recall, but also to be able to apply them to situations. If you have students working in teams, collaboration is also a skill they will be learning. They might work together to find definitions, study, and quiz one another.

How Do You Run This Activity?

I have experienced WordMasters run as an afterschool club, and I have seen ELA teachers use it as part of their curriculum. That is kind of the beauty of the program; there is a lot of flexibility as to how it is run. If you are going to run it as a club, my meetings involved students using their lists to look up words and gain an understanding of them. Sometimes I would have students take part in creative studying, such as creating a FlipGrid video for each of the words that could be used for studying, or they would try to write stories using all of the words on the list. To review, we would sometimes play charades, with students acting out their words. If WordMasters were being done as part of a class, the teacher could give assignments and projects that help students to learn these words.

For more helpful tips, the website has a page that shows ways you can run your WordMasters program, complete with what you should be doing before, during, and after each meet. More information can be accessed at https://www.wordmasterschallenge.com.

America's Battle of the Books

What Is This Activity?

America's Battle of the Books (https://www.battleofthebooks.org) is just what it sounds like: Students are provided with a list of various books that they must read and then battle with others by answering questions about them. The better that students comprehend a book, the better the chance they will be able to answer a question concerning it. Students compete in teams at regional competitions. As the website states:

> *America's Battle of the Books* is a reading incentive program for students. . . . Students read books and come together, usually in groups, to demonstrate their abilities and to test their knowledge of the books they have read. (America's Battle of the Books, n.d., para. 1)

Figure 2 is an example of some of the novels from the 36 books on the elite grades 6–8 list. You can see it is a mix of contemporary and classic nonfiction and fiction. The list gives students a wide variety of choices. Ideally, you would have a team of students, and they would divide the book list up into parts so that

---

FIGURE 2

Battle of the Books Sample Titles for Grades 6–8 Elite List

Title	Author
Anne Frank: Diary of a Young Girl	Anne Frank
Touching Spirit Bear	Ben Mikaelson
City of Ember	Jeanne DuPrau
The Call of the Wild	Jack London
Seabiscuit: An American Legend	Laura Hillenbrand

---

each student is only reading a few books, rather than one student reading them all. Then, three of these students would act as the representatives who compete at the Battle of the Books.

Who Can Be Involved?

There are various categories available. Students as young as second graders reading 64 pages of *Freckle Juice* can compete, as can seniors in high school reading college preparatory books such as *Beowulf*. There are different reading levels within a grade range, so the grades 4–6 lists have a short, medium, standard, and elite list that can be used with your gifted students. The ranges of grades are typically grades 3–5, 4–6, and 7–8. There are also lists for homeschooled children, a Spanish list, and younger and older lists. The teacher/advisor would just need to determine the list that would be most appropriate for their students.

Where Does This Activity Take Place?

Different states and regions decide whether to host a Battle of the Books tournament. It is typically held at a host school, and students from the surrounding area converge at this school to compete as a school team. It is run sort of like a quiz bowl. Students arrive at the Battle of the Books site and play several rounds, answering questions in their category. At the end of several rounds, points are totaled, and the two teams with the most points square off against one another. Depending on how these two teams do, they might be invited to participate in a regional tournament in April, bringing in schools from the area, and then the statewide battle in May. Not all states hold these regional or state events, but regardless, you can run a local Battle of the Books within your school district or county.

When Does This Activity Occur?

The lists are usually released at the beginning of the academic year so that students will have enough time to be able to read the list of books. The dates for these competitions are determined by each state. For instance, Mississippi hosts a state tournament in May, servicing nine different regions in the state.

Why Should Students Participate?

This competition feeds a love of reading. Not only that, the competition forces students to develop better comprehension skills because if they forget what they read, it will be difficult to answer questions about a book. For gifted students, the lists are great because one of the most difficult things to do is find a book at a student's appropriate reading level that is also age appropriate in subject matter. Just because a fourth grader can read at a 10th-grade level doesn't mean you want a 9-year-old reading *The Hunger Games.* These lists do a pretty good job of choosing school-appropriate books that are going to challenge students' reading levels.

How Do You Run This Activity?

I have started with groups as large as 25 students. Typically, I divide them into smaller groups, say of 3–4 students. Students then divvy up the books amongst their group members, and then each student becomes an expert on their books. We spend meetings discussing the books we have read and taking practice comprehension quizzes.

I either provide deadlines for when books should be read, or if you are seeking to teach more responsibility, students can create these timelines themselves. Some students pace themselves very well, some not so much. I had one student who was such a voracious reader that he not only read his assigned books, but also read those of his teammates.

In order to decide who was going to go to the regional Battle of the Books, we would have a club tournament. Students would be on the stage at tables with buzzers that we purchased similar to what they would see at the competition. We invited other classes, parents, and administrators to act as an authentic audience. Part of what you get when you purchase a list of books are questions relating to those books. We would then have teams compete against each other, having a quarterfinal, semifinal, and final. The team that won the final was then invited to attend the regional Battle of the Books, which was held just a few cities away.

The cost of the club is $40 for the starter kit, plus the purchase of books for students to read. If your classroom or school library already has these books, you would not have to worry about this cost.

Finding your regional and state competitions can be challenging, depending on which state you are from. Some competitions are highly organized, while others are not. Unfortunately, there is no central page that links you to all of the states' Battle of the Books information, so you would have to do a Google search to find if there is one in your area. Many times these are sponsored by local libraries. Find out more information at https://www.battleofthebooks.org. Even if there is not a competition in your area, running it at your own school can be very rewarding for students. Just make sure you try to make the culminating experience as authentic as possible.

North American Computational Linguistics Olympiad

What Is This Activity?

The name for the North American Computational Linguistics Olympiad (https://nacloweb.org) is quite a mouthful, but that is the point. Also known as NACLO for short, it is a contest for secondary students in which they solve linguistic puzzles. What exactly is a linguistics puzzle, you might ask? It can look like this:

> **Question 1 (Very difficult).** The sequence of words [dog, ore, get] has the property that taking the nth letter of each word, in order, forms the nth word. For example, the 2nd letters of "dog", "ore", and "get" are 'o', 'r', and 'e', which spell the second word "ore".
>
> Find a sequence of six 6-letter English words (no proper nouns, please!) with the same property.
>
> Hint: one such sequence exists containing the words "spread" and "acetic". (NACLO, n.d.-b)

Participants in the NACLO could be asked several different types of linguistic problems:

- **Translation problems:** A problem includes a set of sentences in a foreign language and their translations into English, which may be in order or out of order. Your task is to learn as much as possible from these translations and then translate other given sentences to or from English.
- **Number problems:** A problem includes foreign sentences that describe basic arithmetic facts, such as "six times four is twenty-four," and your task is to figure out how to translate different numbers and expressions.
- **Writing systems:** Your task is to figure out how a particular writing system works and then use it to write out a given text, such as an ancient inscription. Some languages are written right to left or top to bottom, others do not use vowels, etc.
- **Calendar systems:** Your task is to figure out what calendar was used by a particular civilization based on sentences that refer to it.
- **Formal problems:** You have to build a logical model of a language phenomenon. For example, a transformation rule may say "to convert an active voice sentence to passive voice, make the object of the former sentence the subject of the latter one, convert the verb to passive by using an appropriate form of the verb "to be" with the past participle of the verb, and add "by" before the word that was the subject of the former sentence."
- **Phonological problems:** Your task is to figure out the relationship between the sounds of a language and its writing system.
- **Computational problems:** Your task is to develop a procedure to perform a particular linguistic task in a way that can be carried out by a computer. (NACLO, n.d.-a)

Who Can Be Involved?

NACLO is for students in the 13–18 age range, but you can get permission from the organizers if someone younger wishes to take part. Even if a student does not have a strong sense of linguistics, they can always learn. Prior experience is not necessary to participate. This is an individual competition; however, you could take several students from the same school as long as they are registered.

Where Does This Activity Take Place?

The Open Round, or the first round, can be hosted at two different types of sites—a high school or a university site. The high school site just requires someone, either an advisor or teacher, to supervise the contest at their school. Many universities—including Carnegie Melon, Georgetown, The Ohio State University, Cornell, and Yale—are amongst the nearly 80 colleges that host a NACLO tournament. It does not matter whether it is at a high school or university site. A list of all high school and university sites can be accessed on the competition's website at https://www.nacloweb.org/university_sites.php or https://www.nacloweb.org/high_school_sites.php.

The top students from the Open Round are then invited to the Invitational Round, which has students using an online practice program. From this, the top four American, as well as Canadian, students will be the representatives at the International Linguistics Olympiad. As its name implies, this is usually held in a foreign country. Latvia, Korea, and India were hosts in the past few years. Students who qualify are expected to pay for expenses themselves.

When Does This Activity Occur?

The competition takes place in three parts. The first part is the Open Round, which is open to any students who register online. This typically takes place in January. The Open Round lasts for 3 hours and involves students working on 5–8 problems. These are then judged, and the top scorers are invited to take part in the online Invitational Round. This usually takes place in March. There are generally 6–10 questions that are more challenging than those seen before at the Open Round. The top scorers then qualify for the International Linguistics Olympiad. The host nation sets the date for when this will occur, but it is usually in the summer or into the fall. It is a multiple day event.

Why Should Students Participate?

Being able to manipulate and transform language makes a person a better writer, reader, and speaker of the language. Although linguistics is the focus, the competition involves logical thinking, which is a valuable trait for students to learn and put into practice. For gifted students, who many times come to you with an already advanced vocabulary, this activity merely develops their skills even further and allows them to use their skills in a creative manner.

How Do You Run This Activity?

Students do not have to do any preparation before the competition. They could simply show up on that day and compete. That would not be advisable given the difficulty of the questions. It would be very beneficial for students to be exposed to all of the different types of problems they may encounter at the competition. That is why many high schools and universities offer training sessions for students in the area. These typically involve understanding linguistics and working on practice problems.

However, you want to lend support to your students, so running a weekly meeting might be a good idea so that students can gain an understanding of the types of questions in the competition. You and your students can run through all sorts of practice problems provided by NACLO at https://www.nacloweb. org/resources.php. At these meetings, students could work on these in order to gain an understanding of the format of the various questions, which can be half the battle in preparing for this competition. Even though the actual competition is individual, having students work as a team and help one another to explain the answers and strategies can go a long way in developing confidence and competence for the competition.

Your budget would depend on whether or not you decide to host a tournament or transport students who wish to participate.

Homegrown Idea— Creative Writing Club

What Is This Activity?

You can set up a creative writing club any way you like. Typically, this involves a group of students meeting every so often to talk about writing and the ideas they have for poems and/or stories. A good creative writing club is not run by the advisor but rather the students themselves. The role of the advisor is simply to provide the structure for students to work and making sure the space is a safe one in which students can freely share their work without judgment.

Who Can Be Involved?

You could do this for any grade level, but I recommend gearing it toward higher grade levels, grades 5 and up. This is because creative writing is mostly done independently of class, meaning that although there may be some time during club meetings to write, most of the writing will be done on the students' time. Younger grades would need more support and might incur difficulty while writing independently and not having anyone who can guide them. Also, many of the contests available that students can enter are for older students. You could certainly host this AECA for younger students, but be prepared to be more hands-on and provide students with more direction.

Where Does This Activity Take Place?

Because of the independent nature of this club, you do not have to hold regularly scheduled in-person meetings. You could create a Google Classroom, providing assignments and deadlines, and students could simply share a Google Doc with the group for students to be able to edit and comment. This club works very effectively when students interact with one another, whether in-person or virtually. That is kind of the power of a club like this; it becomes more of a community than a club. Writing can be a very lonely process, and there are many authors who gather with other authors so that they can have someone to talk to. That is what a club like this provides—a space for students to help one another in their writing.

When Does This Activity Occur?

In order for this to work for students, they need to meet somewhat regularly (in-person or virtually) in order to be able to brainstorm ideas with another and workshop their works. When I ran a writing club, I met with students every other week, we talked about the progress of their pieces, and I would remind them of deadlines if there were any. About every other meeting we would have a workshop during which students brought what they had written and peers read each other's works and made suggestions or comments.

Why Should Students Participate?

Because there is such a focus on academic writing in the regular classroom, students do not get the opportunity to use writing for its greatest advantage, which is to express one's creativity and feelings. Creative writing is a great way for students to imagine amazing stories, express emotions, or find their voice. We often do not give students opportunities to find and use their voices in the regular classroom, so having a place they can express themselves is important. Writing also provides gifted students with an outlet for their many and varied thoughts. Many gifted students are abstract thinkers, and focusing their thoughts in a more concrete manner can be a challenge. Writing provides a structured outlet that allows students to creatively express their thoughts.

Students who are interested in writing find out one of two things: Either they discover that writing is more difficult than they thought, and although they might continue to do it as a hobby, they are not going to pursue it in college or the job market, or they may find out writing is what they really want to do. For every story of a John Green who writes a book that becomes a worldwide best-seller, there are millions of writers who cannot even get a foot in the door. It is important to understand the writing process and how it works. I graduated with a degree in creative writing, but my college spent zero time explaining how to prepare a manuscript for submission, how to write a cover letter, or even how to find what market to send it to in the first place. I had to learn this on my own, and even as a published author, I still feel like I do not have a good grasp on the process.

How Do You Run This Activity?

Running the writing club is up to your discretion. For every hourlong meeting we had, I spent 15 minutes going over a skill that was going to benefit students in their writing. This might involve looking at basic story structure, how to write dialogue, how characters are developed, editing, and other writing conventions that would benefit students writing their stories. When we got closer to submitting a piece for publication, I had sessions on formatting and how to write a cover letter. Sometimes I would even have guest authors, who would talk to the group about their writing process and give suggestions for young writers. We had conversations with Alan Gratz, Tyler Whitesides, and Eric Berlin. All I did was email these authors and asked if they could spare any time to talk to my students, and they graciously agreed to Skype so that students could ask questions and interact with the author.

In order to make the writing club more authentic and to give the students some focus, I usually found a writing contest for teens and set our goal for each member of our club to submit an entry. This resource from the Johns Hopkins Center for Talented Youth includes links to several contests that are available to teen creative writers https://cty.jhu.edu/resources/academic-opportunities/competitions/art_writing.html. This provided us with a deadline and something for the students to work toward. When we finally had our pieces ready for submission, to increase the authenticity, we usually had a public reading at a coffee house or at the school, inviting parents and staff to attend.

I tried as much as possible to let the club be student run, including when we would have a meeting where we workshopped a student's piece. This was totally driven by the students and their responses, rather than me evaluating the work. I took part in the discussion as an equal member. Other times I just gave students space to write and brainstorm ideas with one another. However you decide to run it, make sure you keep in mind that a writing club is about students finding their voices, so you have to create a space where they can use them loud and clear.

Something Extra to Think About

No matter which AECA you decide to implement with your students in order to enhance their ELA skills, it is important that they see the love behind it. Students should love to write, they should love linguistics, they should see the love people have for reading, and they should love to play with words. Taking part will feed their love for learning, something that schools need to do a better job of fostering. The club or activity you start might be the only outlet for these students.

CHAPTER **3**

Math

I am not a really big fan of math. For whatever reason, somewhere in my education I found a distaste for it, but I am very aware that there are students and adults out there who love math. One of my best friends was a physics major, and he would get such entertainment and gratification working on a formula that had perplexed him. There is no doubt that math is a very valuable skill to learn. Students will be using math in some form or another in their everyday lives. The problem is that students cannot always see how math applies to the real world. Finding competitions that show students how math can be used in the real world is very important. By competing in an authentic competition and applying math skills to real-world tasks, students can begin to see and understand math's true relevance.

DOI: 10.4324/9781003234982-4

MATHCOUNTS

What Is This Activity?

MATHCOUNTS (https://www.mathcounts.org) is a program that allows students with strong abilities in math to compete against their peers as they solve complex math problems. The program has the same basic format for all four levels of competition. Students and teams compete in four different types of rounds. They are:

- **Sprint Round:** Focuses on speed and accuracy. Students have 40 minutes to complete 30 math problems without a calculator.
- **Target Round:** Focuses on problem solving and mathematical reasoning. Students receive 4 pairs of problems and have 6 minutes to complete each pair, assuming the use of a calculator.
- **Team Round:** Focuses on problem solving and collaboration. Students have 20 minutes to complete 10 math problems, assuming the use of a calculator. Only the 4 students on a school's team can take this round officially.
- **Countdown Round:** Focuses on speed and accuracy. Students have a maximum of 45 seconds per problem without a calculator. This round is optional at the school, chapter and state level. (MATHCOUNTS, n.d.-a)

If you do the math here, these rounds take about a total of 2 hours to complete. Students who are most successful move on to the next round, which could lead to the national competition.

The problems students are tasked with are a little more robust than your typical math problem. This is a benefit of using such a program. Students must not only be precise in their calculations, but also carefully analyze each problem to determine the best process for solving it. Here is an example of a MATHCOUNTS problem:

> Millions of people will fix their eyes on the ball dropping in Times Square this New Year's Eve to indicate the end of 2019 and the beginning of 2020. The famous ball is six feet in diameter and weighs 1070 pounds. If the weight were distributed evenly throughout the ball, what would be the average number of pounds per cubic foot, to the nearest tenth? (Assume that the ball is a perfect sphere, though its surface is actually made up of 504 small, crystal triangles.) (MATHCOUNTS, 2019, para. 1)

Who Can Be Involved?

MATHCOUNTS is for students in grades 6–8. You need to form MATH-COUNTS teams, although students can participate individually. They just would not participate in the Team Round. The cost, as of 2020, is $35 per student.

Where Does This Activity Take Place?

Because MATHCOUNTS takes place on four different levels, the "where" changes from level to level. For instance, the first round is held at the local school. The school advisor administers the test. If students advance to the Chapter Competition, this is usually held at a common site, as chapters cover the entire state. Virginia has eight different chapters so that students from all over the state can participate and compete. To find your closest chapter, visit https://www.math counts.org/dates-locations-and-coordinators. The next level is the state competition, which is held in a major city in the state. Florida's is held in Jacksonville, and Illinois's is in Joliet, just to name a couple. If students are the top four competitors from their state, they are invited to attend the National Competition with all expenses paid for the students and one parent. These four competitors act as a state team at the competition. The location changes from year to year, but it has been held in Orlando, FL, several times over the past decade.

When Does This Activity Occur?

The following is a timeline of events in the MATHCOUNTS process:
- Advisors register in the fall. By doing so, they receive a competition kit.
- The school administers the test around January.
- Students advance to the Chapter Competition in February.
- Top students from the chapter go to state in March.
- The top four individual competitors receive an all-expenses trip to the National Competition in May.

Why Should Students Participate?

The biggest advantage of doing MATHCOUNTS is that many of the problems put math in the real world, helping students to see how they will encounter math in their lives. It is very important to make this connection, so that students can see the relevance of math. A second reason is that it is surprisingly fun. I have been to a MATHCOUNTS competition and watched the Countdown Round. This involves two students competing against one another. The question is posted up on the screen, and students race to be the first to complete it. When I was there, the audience watched in anticipation, some of them attempting the question themselves, and when the winner was announced, the crowd would gasp. It was like we were watching a basketball game.

I often promote magnet programs for gifted students because they put like-minded students together in one place where they can discover that it is alright to be themselves. Similarly, a competition such as this puts like-minded gifted mathematical thinkers together in one place and lets them know there are other people who find math fun. It is important for people to find peers they relate to, whether that be in sports, politics, religion, or math.

How Do You Run This Activity?

The advisor for a MATHCOUNTS club would need to schedule and run practices. This is how students become familiar with the types of problems as well as the thinking behind them. During these meetings, you can work on practice problems as a team and talk through the mathematical concepts. No matter how many students you have participating in the club, you will need to narrow it down to no more than 10 students who get to go to the Chapter Competition. This will be decided when you administer the first round of testing in January.

As for materials to use at meetings, this is exactly the reason using already established national competitions makes things much easier for the advisor. The MATHCOUNTS folks do an excellent job of providing resources and lessons. They suggest the meetings follow this format:

- **Warm-up:** To warm up, Mathletes will start with a short problem set to practice related skills that will be expanded upon throughout the practice plan.
- **The Problems:** To introduce a common type of MATHCOUNTS competition problem and/or a helpful problem-solving strategy, Mathletes will watch a video which solves and explains the approach to two or three problems.
- **Piece It Together:** Building on the warm-up and the video, Mathletes will combine their prior knowledge and the strategies they learned to solve another set of related problems.
- **Optional Extension:** Each practice plan will have an activity, puzzle or game as an option to end with. The extension will be related to the concept the problems explored and give Mathletes an opportunity to have a little fun and/or be creative with the problem-solving skills. (MATHCOUNTS, n.d.-b)

MATHCOUNTS actually provides specific problems for students to use at these meetings. These practice plans can be accessed here: https://www.math counts.org/mathcounts-practice-plans.

Continental Math League

What Is This Activity?

Continental Math League (https://www.cmleague.com) is a math competition that does not require participants to travel anywhere to compete. Students work on problems provided by the Continental Math League (CML) on specific dates, and the teacher grades and submits scores. The category in which students are competing determines the number of meets the teacher will have to administer. There is no restriction as to the number of students who can participate in a given category. If you have a class of 30 students, all 30 can take the test. They just need to complete the problems in a proctored environment where they have a time limit they must adhere to. The top six scores are submitted.

Who Can Be Involved?

Another nice thing about the Continental Math League is that is spans across many ages and grades. There are four types of competitions:
- grades 2–3,
- the Pythagorean or Euclidean Division (grades 4–9),
- Computer Science (grades 3–8), and
- the Calculus League (Advanced Placement students).

The advisor picks the category as well as the grade level. Then they purchase the packet for the contest, usually between $75 and $100, depending on the category. If a school wants several classrooms to be able to participate, each classroom having its own top six scores, additional team packets would need to be purchased.

Where Does This Activity Take Place?

As mentioned previously, this competition takes place in the comfort of your own classroom or school. The advisor must proctor the exam, making sure to adhere to the time limit. The grades 2–3, Pythagorean/Euclidean, and Computer Science competitions all have a 30-minute time cap. The Calculus League gets 40 minutes per meet. Advisors are provided with an answer key that they use to grade and rank the top six scorers. Those scorers who are the highest will receive regional and/or national awards. For each group that participates, the advisor is provided with five certificates and two medals, which can be distributed accordingly.

When Does This Activity Occur?

Each competition has a specific date that each meet must be held. These, of course, change from year to year. Figure 3 is an example. Depending on whether the competition is being done in a math class or is run as a club, the advisor would have to coordinate to make sure there is a block of uninterrupted time for students to perform in the meet. Then, the tests must be graded using the answer key provided and the scores submitted in a timely manner.

Why Should Students Participate?

Math is all about problem solving, and the problems in the Continental Math League are a little more cognitively challenging than typical problems. Problem solving, as I noted, is a valuable 21st-century skill. The value of this skill can be summarized:

> The ability to problem solve is a skill students will use for the rest of their lives. Think about the worth an employee with strong problem-solving skills would be to an employer. After all, solving problems creatively and effectively saves money and leads to new clients. Although it seems at times like those with the ability to problem solve just have an innate ability to do so, somewhere in their experiences they learned this skill. (Stanley, 2018, pp. 20–21)

How Do You Run This Activity?

This sort of club fits nicely into a regular classroom setting when you are trying to challenge students. I have had teachers use it as part of their curriculum, introducing mathematical concepts students may see on the test and working up to the competition date. As with after an exam in all math classes,

FIGURE 3
Sample Continental Math League Schedule

	Meet 1	Meet 2	Meet 3	Meet 4	Meet 5
Grades 2–3	January 3	February 6	March 12		
Calculus	December 5	February 6	March 12	April 23	
Computer Science	January 16	February 12	March 19		
Euclidean and Pythagorean	November 7	December 5	January 9	February 6	March 12

it is important that the advisor reviews the content with students using the step-by-step solutions provided by CML. Through this process, students can learn what they were successful at or receive feedback on and understand their mistakes. This reflection process is how students improve.

This competition could also be run as an afterschool club. At meetings, students could look at practice problems and solve them either individually or work as a team. There are books that can be purchased that contain problems from past CML tests. They can be found at https://www.cmleague.com/product-category/books.

World Maths Day

What Is This Activity?

No, "maths" is not a typo. In most of the world, math is spelled as "maths," and this competition is a global one. World Maths Day is a single-day celebration of mathematics around the world. It involves participants from all over the world playing 60-second games online involving mental math problems. These games test for quickness and accuracy, and students compete against others from around the globe. There are 10 different levels, so you can find an appropriate grade and skill level for challenging students. The competition starts with simple addition problems in Level 1 and goes up to 10, which involves converting units for area and volume. Students get a point for every question they correctly answer, and the person and/or school who gets the most points is the leader. Students spend the entire day trying to crack the leaderboard. There is a 48-hour window in which students can compete (after all, it is World Maths Day somewhere in the world during this time frame).

Who Can Be Involved?

The 10 different levels cover the age ranges of 4 to 16. The advisor just needs to register the class or club and download the competition pack. The program used is known as Mathletics. Part of your subscription allows you to get students ready by participating in the warm-up event.

Where Does This Activity Take Place?

Because the competition is online, students can compete in the comfort of their own classroom. Students compete against each other to see who can get the highest score in the class, but they also compete as a team, meaning if enough individuals get good scores, the team could be on the leaderboard. What is really cool is that students can see how their results compare to students from around the world. More than 4 million students participate in the event from all over the globe.

From these leaders, a number of awards are provided for students. The top 10 students in the world are awarded gold medals, and a champion is crowned.

When Does This Activity Occur?

World Maths Days is a unique competition because everyone is participating on the exact same day. For example, in 2019 World Maths Day was held on March 14. Students come to school and log in to the website. They then compete in a round or a series of rounds and see how their scores compare to others who have taken part. Students can strike out early if they answer three questions wrong.

Why Should Students Participate?

World Maths Day is a celebration of math. There are people from all over the world, all speaking different languages, and yet the common language is that of mathematics. The competition allows students to see children in China or Brazil understanding the same math problems as them without any translation. This helps students see the bigger picture of math and its usefulness, as no matter what the country, 1 + 1 equals 2 and a right angle is always going to be 90 degrees. The competition shows students how math is used to navigate everyday life in everything from business to politics to religion. Math is a shared language that connects us all.

Because you can choose the level of your competition, you can differentiate the event so that students who struggle in math can work with basic concepts while those more gifted in math can be challenged. This competition also shows children that math can be fun and something to look forward to. If you effectively promote the competition in your class or club, students' excitement will build as they event approaches, much like it would in anticipation of a holiday. They are excited when World Maths Day comes and are eager to participate in math activities. There are even World Maths masks that can be downloaded from the resources page to get students in the spirit https://www.worldmaths day.com/resources. Math is not always the most exciting subject area for some students, so using an event such as this to generate excitement can make students who feel so-so about math actually begin to enjoy it.

How Do You Run This Activity?

World Maths Day could be run as part of a regular math class within the school day or as an afterschool club. To get students prepared, you should have students conduct practice rounds where they build up points. You could even make this a competition, with the club leader getting a prize or honor. Doing these practice sessions gets students used to the format of the competition, increases their confidence and speed, and as a bonus helps them to learn valuable math facts.

Once World Maths Day starts, you can choose to have students compete versus the class, the school, or the world. When you choose a level for your students, there are several rounds for each level. Students can begin at the same time and race against the clock, trying to be the fastest to answer correctly. Students have to be careful because once they miss three questions, they are eliminated from the round. Whether you conduct World Maths Day as part of a class or a club, I would certainly hype up the day, making announcements over the PA leading up to it, putting posters in the hallways celebrating it, and on the day, making a big deal of those competing in it. The nice thing is if a student is absent or unable to attend that day, they can be given their login information and they can compete from home. This also means that this is an AECA that could easily be done remotely or in a blended learning situation. You can run each round like a track meet, sounding a buzzer when the round begins and ends. At the end of each round, acknowledge the students who got the highest scores. There are certificates you can print out and give to the winners of rounds (see https://www.worldmathsday.com/resources).

You will not get final placement of the class or individual students until after the competition. The organization will tabulate the winners, and a number of awards are offered to the students who take part and for those who do well in the event. Additionally, the champions and the top 10 students in the world are awarded gold medals every year. Mathletics is free for the month of March, which is when the competition takes place. If you want to use it before then or build on their skills after, you have to pay to continue your access after the event.

MathWorks Math Modeling Challenge

What Is This Activity?

MathWorks Math Modeling (M3) Challenge (https://m3challenge.siam.org) bills itself as a different kind of math contest, which is why I included it here. The competition does not go through as many calculations as some other contests in this chapter. Instead, the competition asks for a tangible solution to a real-world problem. In other words, it requires students to be able to use their mathematical abilities to figure out a problem in an authentic situation:

> Teams are presented with a previously unknown problem scenario, and should work together, using the math modeling process to represent, analyze, make predictions, and otherwise provide insight into that real-world phenomena and the posed problem's questions. (Society for Industrial and Applied Mathematics, n.d., para. 1)

This challenges students' mathematical thinking. And because they are applying it to a real-world situation, there is no one definitive answer. Different teams could arrive at different results, which is what makes the math authentic. The team is scored on the following:
- using mathematical models either developed originally or discovered through research,
- demonstrating a depth of understanding of their solution, and
- providing additional insight if their solution is drawn from sources (Society for Industrial and Applied Mathematics, 2018, para. 1).

To create their models, teams need to:
- define all variables and parameters (with units),
- justify assumptions,

- describe the mathematical approaches used in the model,
- apply to or demonstrate for any situations presented, and
- discuss implications of the results (Society for Industrial and Applied Mathematics, 2018, para. 2).

Who Can Be Involved?

This is a contest for high school students, specifically juniors and seniors. Schools must form teams of three to five students, and can have two teams maximum competing. All participants on a team must be from the same school. They work on a problem that requires math modeling. Here is an example from a past competition:

BETTER ATE THAN NEVER
Reducing Wasted Food[1]

The Food and Agriculture Organization of the United Nations reports that approximately one third of all food produced in the world for human consumption every year goes uneaten.

As an example, perfectly good produce that is considered misshapen or otherwise unattractive is regularly discarded before reaching your grocery store shelves. Uneaten food also wastes resources (water, fertilizer, pesticides, land, etc.) used in food production. At the same time, it has been estimated that over 42 million Americans are food-insecure and could take advantage of all of this squandered food, frequently described as "wasted food."

Create a mathematical model that a state could use to determine if it could feed its food-insecure population using the wasted food generated in that state.

Personal choices when it comes to food consumption primarily occur at the grocery store, school cafeteria, restaurants, and at home. Create a mathematical model that can be used to determine the amount of food waste a household generates in a year based on their traits and habits. Demonstrate how your model works by evaluating it for the following

1 *Note.* Used with permission from MathWorks Math Modeling (M3) Challenge, a scholarship-awarding contest for high school students since 2006. Find this 2018 Challenge problem along with winning solutions, other archival information, and complete information about M3 Challenge at https://m3challenge.siam.org.

BETTER ATE THAN NEVER, continued

households (provided data may be helpful):
- Single parent with a toddler, annual income of $20,500
- Family of four (two parents, two teenage children), annual income of $135,000
- Elderly couple, living on retirement, annual income of $55,000
- Single 23-year-old, annual income of $45,000

Your submission should include a one-page executive summary with your findings, followed by your solution paper—for a maximum of 20 pages.

Where Does This Activity Take Place?

This competition takes place wherever the students decide to work. They download the problem from the website on a given weekend, and as soon as that happens, the clock starts ticking and the team must submit their final solution within 14 hours. Teams are not allowed to have any outside help with the solution, including the coach. In fact, it is not necessary for the advisor to be present during the 14-hour window. The team must produce a typed solution paper, no longer than 20 pages, which builds their written communication skills. It must include elements such as a summary, restatement of the problem, analysis, design of the model, discussion, citations, etc.

Each year has a set theme. Some past years' themes include substance use and abuse, the national park service, modeling new approaches to mobility, the value of a college education, and recycling.

When Does This Activity Occur?

Teams have a registration deadline sometime in February. When students register, they are given a 14-hour work time, which can be done between Friday at 8 a.m. and Monday at 8 p.m. The team could decide to schedule this a certain way depending on resources and availability. One option is that you have a math overnighter at the school, during which the team works on the problem until the 14-hour time limit has lapsed. Or, if you started a Saturday or Sunday morning at 7 a.m., the competition window would be over by 11 p.m. It would be near impossible to fit this into a normal day's schedule because school does not normally last for 14 hours. You could certainly start it during the school day, say at 9 a.m., and then students would burn the midnight oil until 1 a.m. the following day. Although I would not recommend starting 14 hours before the deadline of the competition, because it closes at 8 p.m. on Monday, you could have students come into school at 4 a.m. that morning. No matter what time you decide to begin, the clock cannot be paused for any reason.

Why Should Students Participate?

Any chance to show students how math can be used in the real world is always a really good thing. Mathematical modeling does just that, requiring students to use mathematical concepts to make predictions or provide insight into real-world phenomena. It is also very cross-curricular. Yes, students must use math to try and solve the problem, but then they must write their rationale for why they made the choices they did and communicate through writing. Many of the issues the problems focus on involve social studies, such as making sense of the U.S. Census or solving the Social Security problem, or science in trying to predict how a flu outbreak will affect the U.S. or decide whether a high-speed train would be beneficial.

Because this competition involves more mathematical thinking than just math facts, those students who are gifted in math will be provided with problems that allow them to go a bit deeper. There is also more than one possible answer, so students get to use the higher levels of thinking of Bloom's taxonomy, including analyzing, evaluating, and creating. It is these levels of critical thinking that challenge gifted students.

In addition to the educational advantage comes the monetary one. The challenge does not cost anything to participate in, yet teams who achieve Honorable Mention, Semi-Finalist, Finalist, or Technical Computing Awardee status can win scholarships. The winners in 2020 received $20,000. The M3 Finalist and Technical Computing Awardee teams are also invited to New York, NY, for the final event, all expenses paid.

How Do You Run This Activity?

First and foremost, students need to gain a full understanding of what mathematical modeling looks like and how it works. Fortunately, the M3 website has provided an abundance of resources in order to teach students. There is a 72-page handbook for free online (see https://m3challenge.siam.org/resources/modeling-handbook), as well as a series of videos that not only show you how to teach modeling, but also break down the various parts that will be used for the competition (see https://m3challenge.siam.org/resources/teaching-modeling-videos).

After showing students what mathematical modeling is, they can use this concept to solve the plethora of sample problems found at https://m3challenge. siam.org/resources/sample-problems. Not only are there problems to solve, but also there is an extensive archive of all of the solutions from the past 15 years. Students can analyze these solutions and see what sort of thinking was used in successful entries.

As for what specifically the advisor would be responsible for, the organizers have even laid out a checklist of all of the things you would need to do to get students ready for the M3 Challenge. This can be accessed at https://m3challenge. siam.org/participate/challenge-checklist.

Homegrown Idea—Stock Market Club

What Is This Activity?

People who are involved in the stock market are using math on a daily basis—math to make decisions about how affordable their stock is, math to predict where they think the stock may go, math to determine whether they were profitable or not. A stock market club could be designed for students to play the stock market safely to get an idea of how it works while using math. This could be over the course of a month, a semester, or even an entire school year. Students can create a stock portfolio and then determine at the end who was the most successful with their decisions.

Who Can Be Involved?

I imagine this would be a club for older students because not many elementary children have a budding interest in the stock market. It could start in middle school or junior high levels, but become more complex as an offering to high school students. Because students are playing with house money, they do not need to worry so much about taking risks, but they can learn how to use math to make decisions less risky in order to have more success.

Where Does This Activity Take Place?

This would not be a club that crescendos into a final performance. Rather this would be an accumulation across the entirety of the year. The club would have to establish parameters, such as the amount of money provided to invest, what it looks like when students sell or acquire other stocks, and how long the simulation will last. This could be held in any classroom as long as students have access to the Internet to be able to research stocks and see how much they are selling for.

It would be nice to have a year-end event to showcase the learning that students did over the course of the club. This could be set up as a competition in which students try to sell their portfolios to potential investors, or students give a presentation on what stocks were successful for them and why, or they could make projections for what they believe their stocks will do in a long-term forecast. It would be more authentic if this year-end event were done outside of the school premises and hours. It could be held at a bank, a business center, or the local library, but getting students out into the real world and inviting an authentic audience (such as local business members, bankers, or financial planners, as well as parents and friends) makes it feel more genuine.

When Does This Activity Occur?

This would be a club that would need a decent amount of time to see how the stocks perform. Although a stock might go up or down over the course of a month, to really understand how the stock market works you would need a much longer period to work with. Ideally, this would be a club that could be started at the very beginning of the school year and last through to the end of said school year. If you did have a culminating activity, it would need to be at the end of the year to allow time to see real change in the stock market and thus have more data to analyze.

Why Should Students Participate?

As mentioned before, when students can see math being used in the real world in order to perform authentic tasks, it is going to help them to see the context of what math they are learning as well as the relevance of it. A club such as this would also give students a chance to take part in an authentic activity that most kids their age do not normally partake in. Learning how finances work, understanding what affects the market, and experiencing mistakes without fear of repercussions are all valuable lessons that can be applied to their own lives and used in their adult years.

More than that, students who are gifted in math can see how their abilities can lead to a real-world job role, such as working as an actuary, financial analyst, statistician, market research analyst, economist, or accountant.

How Do You Run This Activity?

At the beginning of the club you would want to give a brief overview of what the stock market looks like. Depending on how knowledgeable you are about the stock market, it might be a good idea to have a guest speaker, such as a financial planner or a stock broker, come in and provide a simplified summary of how it works and how people use it to make money. There are also some basic videos online, such as at https://www.youtube.com/watch?v=p7HKvqRI_Bo or https://www.youtube.com/watch?v=bl797s8u0QQ.

Then, provide students with a budget. You can create whatever guidelines you would like, but it might look something like this:

- Each student begins with $10,000.
- Each student must invest in 4–6 stocks.
- A 3% commission is to be paid for every stock transaction (buying or selling a stock).
- Each student should keep a journal of their activities and thoughts, and a transaction history of all buys and sells. In addition, the student is responsible for keeping track of the current portfolio's market value.

The group could meet weekly, every other week, or even once a month. If you meet too frequently, it does not give stocks enough time to fluctuate, and there is not much math to do. During these meetings, there are many things that can be done:

- Update gains and losses from the last tabulation.
- Sell one of the stocks and purchase a new one in its place.
- Talk about the trends in the market and speculate why some stocks might have gone up while others went down.
- Bring in guest speakers to further student knowledge of investing, such as a banker, or visit places like a brokerage firm.
- Look at past performance of the market, such as during the Wall Street Crash of 1929, Black Monday in 1987, or the Financial Crisis of 2008. Run simulations as to whether these could have been prevented or not.
- Read and discuss a book on investing.
- Watch programs about investing in the stock market, such as *Mad Money*.

How you end the club is up to you, but as discussed, having an authentic performance, whether it be a *Shark Tank* in which students try to convince investors to buy their portfolios, or a portfolio and explanation of the trends they saw over the year to their parents. No matter what you do, you need to have students sell their stocks and report on their portfolio's value, as well as what they personally learned about the market from the experience.

Something Extra to Think About

Showing students how exciting math can be can go a long way in growing passion about the subject amongst students. Competitions can help students care about math because there is a real-world consequence when they do not solve a problem correctly or fully understand a concept. Suddenly, math is not this abstract thing you learn about with lots of theories and ideas—it is concrete and being used to solve real problems. The value of math is clearly shown.

CHAPTER 4

Science

There has been a really big STEM movement in the past decade or so in education, taking science from something done in laboratories behind closed doors to something with widespread practical applications. Extracurricular activities involving science have followed suit. There are many STEM-related camps now offered to students, as well as competitions centered around science, technology, engineering, and math. Take, for instance, the growing number of robotics teams in schools. There are many different competitions, but the biggest is the VEX Robotics Competition, with more than 20,000 teams registering every year, even being televised by ESPN and CBS. In this competition, Teams must construct a robot that can perform certain tasks, program it, and then guide it with a remote control against other robots. Teams learn many valuable 21st-century skills during this process, such as problem solving, critical thinking, collaboration, and the ability to code, which is continuing to grow as a useful skill in the workplace.

DOI: 10.4324/9781003234982-5

Invention Convention

What Is This Activity?

Invention Convention (https://inventionconvention.org/home-page) is a way to "introduce your students to a world in which they will solve their own problems and gain the confidence and 21st-century skills to invent their own future" (Invention Convention, n.d., para. 4).

Invention Convention involves students coming up with an invention that solves a problem, but it does not involve just coming up with the idea. Students must envision what the invention will look like, create a model so that others can see their vision, and then explain how it works to others. It usually breaks down into four parts:

1. journal,
2. design,
3. model, and
4. presentation.

The journal involves students capturing the thought process they went through while developing their invention. This is everything from the initial brainstorming to the refinement to the final product. The journal is very helpful for taking the grandiose ideas that students begin with and funneling them into a more practical solution that can be worked on. The journal can be downloaded from the organization's website.

Students must then take the idea that has been floating around in their heads and conceptualize what it will look like. Students start first by drawing what the invention might look like, including its dimensions and what materials it is made of. From this design, students construct a model of the invention. It does not have to be a working model; it simply needs to give people an idea of how it might work. For example, one year I had a student come up with an invention for an alarm lamp. The premise was simple; instead of the alarm going off and blaring a noise, it merely turned on a lamp, which was a more effective way to wake this student up. In order to demonstrate this, my student took an old lamp from his house and affixed a LED clock display to it. It didn't work, but it gave the judges a good idea how it would look.

I have had students create fully functional models, such as a student whose invention was a llama hair rake that separated the hair from the rake tongs. He would even put llama hair from the farm he helped his parents run, on the ground and demonstrate how it worked. But an actual working model does not gain an advantage over someone's model that does not. Students can even substitute materials that make it easier for them to work with. For instance, we would not expect a fourth grader to be able to weld together pieces of metal if that is what the invention would be made of. Instead, that student could tape pieces of cardboard together to represent the same thing.

The final aspect is presenting the invention. Although it is not required, a majority of students create trifolds chronicling the process of how they came up with and developed their invention. This acts as a visual aid to demonstrate to judges what the student is talking about. I have learned that spending a lot of time helping students work on the presentation aspect is important because, even if a student creates an amazing idea, if they cannot communicate their idea clearly to a judge, then their invention will not score as well. I always use the example of how Thomas Edison was a master explainer, which is why he is credited with so many inventions even though most of them were developed by teams of inventors.

I have been doing Invention Convention for more than 20 years, and even though it sounds very STEM-like, it came about before the STEM movement gained traction. I liked it because it was very practical, and more importantly, it really did not involve a lot of hardcore science, meaning students were not going to be turned away because they did not possess the scientific knowledge. Students did not necessarily need to know how their invention worked—they just had to have the imagination so that someone else could build it. It was about imagining an idea and then communicating how to bring that idea to life. Because of this, I can do Invention Convention with students as young as kindergartners, but it also remains complex enough that it can be challenging to high school students. The program services K–12 and splits into different divisions so that students are competing with children their own age.

Where Does This Activity Take Place?

Invention Convention takes place at three different levels. For each of these levels, the student is not creating a new invention, but rather presenting the same invention. They may choose to improve some aspects from level to level, but their basic premise stays the same.

The first level is the district level. This is necessary if you have multiple students participating, for there are only a few spots to the state event. The number of spots available usually depends on how many students in the district are taking part. For example, if you have 50 students who are presenting their invention at the district level, only nine of those might qualify for state. At the district level, the advisor is typically responsible for arranging for judges to come in and score students on their invention and the presentation of it.

Top scores move on to the state competition. The state competition is usually a single event where students are first blind judged, which means the judges come around and look at the student journal, model, and display board without the inventor present. Then the second round involves judges coming around and students explaining their inventions with the judges asking questions about them.

Students find out if they qualify for the national competition through an invitation. The competition has been held in Washington, DC, and most recently at the Henry Ford Museum in Dearborn, MI.

When Does This Activity Occur?

The timeline for each state can be different. The district competition can be scheduled anytime the school sees fit, although I usually scheduled mine in April, which is usually a week before the deadline for the state competition applicants. I do this to provide students with more time to work on their inventions. There are other states that hold their state competition earlier (Tennessee's is in February, and California's is in April), meaning their district conventions would have to be held much earlier.

The state Invention Convention depends on when each state decides to hold its competition. I am from Ohio, and it always takes place in the summer so that student work can be displayed at the Ohio State Fair. New York holds its in May in Buffalo at the Museum of Science, while Georgia has one in March at Georgia Tech.

The Nationals have been going on for about 5 years, usually held in the beginning of June. Unlike the state competition there is a cost, including a $300 student registration fee. Do keep in mind, however, that students who are invited are not required to go, so students and families could choose to end their journey at the state competition. To find out exactly when your state hosts its Invention Convention, visit https://inventionconvention.org/local-programs.

Why Should Students Participate?

The main reason I began doing Invention Convention with my students was because I loved the fact that it allows them to be creative. I am always amazed at some of the great ideas students come up with—ideas that should have been invented long ago, but required a fresh look at something to come up with a new concept. At the same time, students must fit their creativity within the confines of reality. For instance, every year I always have students who want to invent a robot that does their homework. We talk about whether this would even be possible, as well as what benefit students would get from someone else doing their homework. I encourage my students to focus on the problem. The problem is kids want help with their homework. Could they come up with an invention that helps kids with their homework while at the same time allowing them to reap the benefits of doing it? Then, students start to think about organizers that might keep a student on task, an alarm that reminds a student to do their homework, or an online forum students can visit to ask questions if they are having trouble. Kids still get to be creative, but they have to understand how their invention fits into the real world and provides an actual benefit.

I always introduced Invention Convention with my gifted students because it helps them to take the abstract, where many gifted students reside in their thinking, and be guided to a more concrete understanding that can actually be used. I also like using it with gifted students because it requires them to respond to the "why." Oftentimes, students who can generate an answer quickly can tell you the "what" but neglect the "why." Think about a student who gives the correct math answer but does not show their work. It is difficult sometimes to get them to understand that the "why" is as, if not more, important than the "what." The process is where the learning takes place, not the outcome.

How Do You Run This Activity?

I have run Invention Convention in various ways. At one point it was part of my sixth-grade science curriculum, so every student in my class participated. Other years it has been run as a club or leadership team. Ideally, you would start it toward the beginning of the school year. I had one-hour meetings with students about every other week. My schedule looked a lot like Figure 4.

I would say the most challenging part is getting students to take the brainstorming and funnel it into something useable. I spend a lot of my introductory time, especially with younger students, trying to take their very grandiose ideas and make them more realistic. I always have students who want to invent a potion that allows people to fly or a pill that stops bullying. I have to work with these students to look at the problem they want to solve and then come up with a more practical solution.

FIGURE 4
Sample Invention Convention Schedule

October 10	Introduction
October 31	Brainstorming
November 7–November 21	Working on journal
December 19–January 9	Creating design of invention
January 23–February 6	Designing model
February 20–March 5	Creating tri-fold
March 19–April 2	Creating presentation
April 16	Finishing touches

FIRST LEGO League

What Is This Activity?

FIRST LEGO League (https://www.firstlegoleague.org) is a multidisciplinary program that combines engineering, computer programming, problem solving, research, presenting, and teamwork into an intense 8-week period. It is a robotics competition in which teams work to build and program a robot to complete a number of tasks on a competition table. Teams compete in a sports-like environment in which spectators cheer their successes. Teams also meet with Robot Design Judges, who evaluate their robot design, programming, and their problem-solving strategies. FIRST LEGO League is a good starting point for schools that want to get into robotics.

Who Can Be Involved?

FIRST LEGO is intended for students ages 9 to 14. Teams consist of 2–10 children. Every year, FIRST LEGO releases a Challenge, which is based on a real-world scientific topic. Each Challenge has three parts: the Robot Game, the Innovation Project, and the Core Values. Teams participate in the Challenge by programming a robot to score points on a themed playing field (Robot Game), developing a solution to a problem they have identified (Project). Teams may then attend an official tournament, hosted by FIRST LEGO Convention Partners.

New teams can expect to pay approximately $800, which includes team registration, the Challenge Set, and a robot kit of parts. There could be additional costs for event participation, travel, food, team shirts, etc.

Where Does This Activity Take Place?

There are a few levels to the competition. First is the regional qualifier. These are typically spread throughout the state. You can find where your nearest regional qualifier is located by going to https://www.firstlegoleague.org/find-first. After that comes the state championship. Eventually the best teams from each state are invited to the World Festival. This is held in multiple cities that rotate every year.

When Does This Activity Occur?

Every year there is a different challenge which is announced in August. Past challenges have included nanotechnology, climate, quality of life for the handicapped population, and transportation. Regional qualifiers are then held throughout the state, so which one is closest to you determines when this will be, but it is usually between November and December. Then there is a district qualifier that takes places in January. This leads into the state championship in February, during which teams can qualify for the World Festival. Figure 5 is an example schedule.

Why Should Students Participate?

FIRST LEGO is a stepping stone to more advanced robotics. Because FIRST LEGO works with kits and because most kids have been putting together LEGO bricks since they were toddlers, there is a certain familiarity with them. Once students begin to become comfortable with this type of robotics, they can graduate to more advanced programs. FIRST even has its own program for high school students called FIRST Robotics.

FIRST LEGO allows students to:
- Research challenges facing today's scientists
- Design, build, test and program robots using technology
- Apply real-world math and science concepts
- Learn critical thinking, team-building, and presentation skills
- Participate in real-world application at tournaments (FIRST LEGO League, n.d.)

FIGURE 5
Sample FIRST LEGO League Schedule

May	Registration Opens
August 1	Global Challenge Release
Late September–Early October	Team Registration Closes
November–March	Tournament Season
April	World Festivals

When students are engaged in hands-on STEM experiences, they build confidence, grow their knowledge, and develop habits of learning. Students are encouraged to try, fail, and try again, while connecting STEM concepts to real-world examples.

How Do You Run This Activity?

There is no generalized time commitment, but I recommend that teams meet at least once per week throughout the season, perhaps even twice per week for 60–90 minutes per meeting. Students should also spend some time outside of practice working on their project, presentation materials, or other team needs. As the Regional Qualifying tournaments approach, many teams choose to meet more frequently to prepare.

FIRST LEGO recommends at least two coaches per team. There are tutorials in the coaches' corner to help you form a team and then coach them properly. These can be found at http://flltutorials.com/CoachCorner.html. FIRST LEGO even provides you with an idea of what the budget for a start-up team would be at https://www.firstinspires.org/robotics/fll/challenge/pricing-and-payment.

Probably one of the more important tasks a coach must do when first starting up a team is to provide the table used for the competition. Here is a plan for building such a table: https://www.firstinspires.org/sites/default/files/uploads/resource_library/fll/table-build.pdf. There are tutorials on how to do this, including a very cool YouTube video that shows a team building theirs through time lapse (see https://www.youtube.com/watch?v=G4fgDoaX_Gk). It is important to have one of these tables because this is what they will be using at the competition. Once you make one, though, it can be used from year to year.

There are many resources for coaching (see https://www.firstinspires.org/resource-library/fll/team-management-resources), including first steps, how the competition is judged, and what to expect at the competition.

Future City Competition

What Is This Activity?

The Future City Competition (https://futurecity.org) is a project-based learning competition that involves students designing and building a city of the future. This means determining the infrastructure for the city that makes it livable as well as incorporating the challenge for that year into the construction of the city. Some past challenges have included building an age-friendly city that involved engineering "two innovative solutions that allow your city's senior citizens to be as active, independent, and engaged as they want to be" (Future City Competition, n.d.-a), and designing a city with a reliable water supply (Future City Competition, n.d.-e).

Teams must design their city to meet the needs of the challenge. It breaks down into five parts:

1. virtual city design,
2. city essay,
3. city model,
4. city presentation, and
5. project plan.

During all phases of the project, students also work with a mentor, typically an engineering student, an architect, or someone who can offer expert advice. It is usually up to the team manager to help find people to act as a mentor.

Once the team has completed all of the phases, they bring all of their materials to the regional competition and are judged on their merits.

Who Can Be Involved?

Future City Competition is for students who are in grades 6–8. A team can be anywhere from three students to 30. If you decide to use a large group, all of the students can be involved in the planning aspect of the city. However, when it comes time to present all of this work to the judges, there are only three students allowed to act as the official presenting team. It might be better off to take those

30 students and form 10 teams of three. This way students can be more directly involved in making decisions. I've had groups as large as 10 students, and what seemed to happen is one student would get mad because another student made a decision without consulting the full group, or there was not enough to do to split the work evenly, so someone got left out. That many students in a single team just seemed more difficult to manage.

Where Does This Activity Take Place?

There are two different levels to Future City. First there is a Regional Competition. This is hosted in most states in a single city, the exceptions being Florida, Texas, California, New York, and Pennsylvania, which have multiple sites. These are held on a Saturday in January, during a 3-week window (depending on the state) starting the second week of the month. These are usually held in large cities such as Boise, ID, Oklahoma City, OK, Knoxville, TN, and Milwaukee, WI, just to name a few. Check on the Future City Competition website for an updated list of where each state's competition is being held.

Finals take place in mid-February in Washington, DC. Once your state identifies you as the winner of the Regional Competition, your team is provided with transportation and hotel accommodations for the three team members presenting, the advisor, and even the mentor.

When Does This Activity Occur?

Most teams register in the spring or summer and then get to work once the school year begins. The competition breaks down into five parts with different due dates for each. These include (Future City Competition, n.d.-b):
1. **Virtual City Design:** Using SimCity, students show their city's progress. They take pictures of their city at various points of its development and then make a slideshow out of these. This is usually due in November or December.
2. **City Essay:** The team must write a 1,500-word essay in which they describe what makes their future city unique and how they solved the challenge given by the Future City Competition. This is also typically due around November or December.
3. **Project Plan:** The team creates a project plan that is due one week before the Regional Competition. This is designed to keep them organized and focused.
4. **City Model:** After showing what the city looks like in SimCity and describing how it works in the essay, students spend the rest of the time

leading up to the regional making a physical model of the city. This does not need to be the entire city but rather a section of it, and it must be a scale model. The requirements are the materials used must be recyclable and include at least one moving part.

5. **City Presentation:** At the Regional Competition, groups must give a 7-minute presentation in which they explain their model and the decisions they made to try to solve the challenge. Afterward, the team should be prepared to answer questions from the judges.

Why Should Students Participate?

The one thing I found that students do not really understand about cities is the infrastructure—that all of those powerlines they see have to run from an electrical plant and into their houses without a gap, the fact that water comes on when they turn on the faucet, that when you go down a road it actually leads to somewhere, and how if you call 911, someone will be there fairly quickly. These all have to do with the setup of the city and the infrastructure that has been established. This is a tough concept for middle school students to grasp but one that Future City teaches really well. This competition will cause students to have a greater appreciation for what is around them and what their community provides, as well as notice things around them that went unnoticed before.

In addition to this, Future City Competition (n.d.-d) allows students to:

- learn how to use engineering to solve real-world problems,
- see how math and science are important to their futures,
- see themselves becoming engineers,
- become comfortable working in a self-directed way, and
- see that they can create something on their own.

The competition also helps build 21st-century skills, including real-world problem solving, time management, public speaking skills, and information literacy. These are skills that will transcend the classroom and be used by the student the rest of his life. What employer wouldn't want someone who manages their time well, or can present information in a clear manner, or solves problems that could save the company a lot of money? Skills such as these make students very valuable in the working world.

These are skills beneficial to gifted students who have problems with executive functioning, such as issues with flexible thinking and self-control. This competition requires a lot of flexible thinking as well as organizational skills that will help these students to learn strategies to overcome these issues.

Another bonus is that Future City Competition is a relatively cheap AECA. It only costs $25 to participate, which includes two copies of the SimCity software. There may be additional costs for materials, but groups are not permitted to spend more than $100.

How Do You Run This Activity?

Future City Competition (n.d.-c) requires the facilitator to have an understanding of two skills:

- the engineering design process that helps teams to design and build their solution, and
- project management to help ensure team projects stay on track.

The competition breaks down into four parts and models the engineering design process:

1. **Define:** During this stage, the team will identify the problem they wish to solve and build background knowledge on how to solve the problem.
2. **Plan:** This stage involves the team trying to develop possible solutions and choosing the best one. Once this vision is in mind, the team will plan out how they will complete it. This involves creating a schedule, assigning roles, and identifying any resources that would be needed.
3. **Do:** This is where the ideas start to come to life. This involves building the model and coming up with the presentation for it.
4. **Review:** This is the reflection of the work in which the team's work is shared and the team determines what lessons they learned (Future City Competition, n.d.-c).

Future City Competition does a pretty decent job of breaking the process down and providing you with what to do at each step. You can request a handbook on the competition's website. In addition to advising the group, you would also be responsible for procuring a mentor for the team. This could be an engineer or engineering student who would help students refine their ideas and provide feedback to the group about their choices.

Science Olympiad

What Is This Activity?

Science Olympiad (https://www.soinc.org) has 15-member teams taking part in different events. In fact, there are 23 team events, falling under five different categories:

1. life, personal, and social science;
2. earth and space science;
3. physical science and chemistry;
4. technology and engineering; and
5. inquiry and nature of science.

The actual events change from year to year, but they all fall under one of these categories. These categories are rotated to reflect the constantly evolving fields of science, such as chemistry, mechanical engineering, genetics, technology, and others.

Science Olympiad involves three types of competition. Knowledge-based usually involves having two participants from the team taking part in a test or analyzing data. An example would be the anatomy and physiology event, which can look like this:

> Teams of two will answer questions concerning anatomy and physiology of the cardiovascular, lymphatic, and excretory systems. They even may be run in stations, as a PowerPoint exam, or simply a test packet.

The next type of event is hands-on. This involves two team members performing experiments or interacting with objects in order to achieve a task. An example here would be experimental design:

> Teams have 50 minutes to design an experiment using provided equipment and are scored on how well-written and thorough their lab report is.

The final type of event is an engineering-based event. This can have two to three team members participating, and they must build a device based on specific criteria and then test their device against others'. One of the more popular events is the Write It Do It:

One team member has to build a device using only the instructions that their teammate wrote about a prebuilt device. The team whose device looks like the closest to the prebuilt device is the winner.

Who Can Be Involved?

Science Olympiad as a competition is designed for students in grades 6–12. There is a division A, which is for elementary students, kindergarten through fifth grade. The events for this division typically only take place at your own school and do not progress to the state or national level. The two other divisions are B and C. B is for middle school students grades 6–9, and C is the high school division, grades 9–12.

The actual school club can have as many members as you like. Some have more than 75 students. However, the team is only allowed to bring 15 participants to take part in the events at a Science Olympiad competition. The other members of the group can help with the preparation, or be mentored by the students who are participating so that they may be ready the following year. You'll notice there is an overlap between the middle and high school divisions. For a middle school team, there can be no more than five ninth graders on the 15-person team. The high school team, on the other hand, cannot have more than seven 12th graders on its team. A ninth-grade student may not participate in both the B and C divisions.

Where Does This Activity Take Place?

Science Olympiad has multiple levels of competition—invitational, regional, state, and national. The invitational is an unofficial tournament and acts as preparation for the regional and state events, exposing students to the formatting and identifying who is ready for the competition.

Each state determines its number of regional tournaments, which act as the gateway to gain acceptance to the state tournament. For instance, Arizona has two regional tournaments, while Michigan has 14 regionals. These regionals are hosted by high schools and colleges. Here is an example of the list of Illinois's 10 regional tournaments:

- February 22: Western Illinois University
- February 29: Neuqua Valley High School
- February 29: Oakton Community College
- March 7: Parkland College
- March 7: Harper College

- March 7: College of Lake County
- March 14: College of DuPage
- March 14: Belleville East High School
- March 14: Illinois Institute of Technology
- March 21: Rock Valley College (Illinois Science Olympiad, n.d.)

You can find where your closest regional competition is held by going to your state's website for Science Olympiad, which can be accessed at https://www.soinc.org/join/state-websites.

Top teams from the regional tournaments then advance to the state tournament. State tournaments are typically hosted at universities. For example, Texas has its at Texas A&M University, and Kansas has its at Wichita State University. Some states, such as New York, split the B and C competitions into two sites. In 2019, New York hosted B at East Syracuse-Minoa High School while C was at LeMoyne College. California breaks its state into northern and southern regions, each with its own state tournament. The state tournament is where the competition is narrowed down to the top one or two teams in your state, which go on to compete in the national competition.

The national tournament has 60 teams competing in the two divisions for a total of 120 teams. It is a 2-day event held at a different university every year. In past years the tournament has been held at universities like North Carolina State University, Cornell University, Colorado State University, etc.

When Does This Activity Occur?

Because invitationals do not officially count as a competition for access into the state tournament, these can be held at any time. Most are held in January or February in order to get teams ready for the regional competitions, which are in late February. There are some, however, that take place earlier or later in the year.

The regional competitions occur from late February to mid-March, depending on when the state tournament is scheduled. The state tournaments are usually held in April—some early in the month, while others are later. This leads into the national tournament that is held in May.

Why Should Students Participate?

Unlike other events in this chapter that focus on STEM and engineering, Science Olympiad has a variety of all sorts of different sciences, including earth and space science, inquiry and nature of science, social science, technology and engineering, and more. There is something for everyone amongst these categories, meaning that someone who loves science can find a way to use their skills in a productive way. This competition also exposes students to a lot of different fields of science. Students could go into the field of medicine with anatomy and physiology, forensics, geology, archeology, medical research, genetics, weather, astronomy, and engineering through many subcategories of the competition.

In addition, students really learn collaboration because no one person can win at Science Olympiad. It must be a team effort, with only two members able to compete in each category. An advisor for this group would have to determine how to spread their 15 group members amongst the many events. That is what practices and invitationals are used for: to determine which members excel at which category.

How Do You Run This Activity?

The Science Olympiad site has suggestions for advisors new to the competition. Here is some of their advice:

> At the beginning of the school year, ask your principal or PTA president for funding for a science extracurricular activity. Tell them you are volunteering to be the coach, and hold an information meeting at PTA, or call a parent/student session in the auditorium. Show a Science Olympiad DVD, put up the list of events for the year with short descriptions, and ask kids to ascertain their interest in the 23 events. Some teachers post lists around the room and have kids sign up for as many events as they find interesting. Once you've got team and parent interest, you're ready to go. Set up a practice schedule—maybe once every other week to start. Assign kids to events, and begin preparations.
>
> Depending on your level of expectation from your team, plan accordingly. Normally, in the first year, it's exciting just to attend a regional tournament. The kids can get their feet wet, see what it's like at a real competition, and scope out the other teams. Plan to meet once a week or more in the months leading up to the tournament. Schedule some study sessions outside of school on the weekends, but remember to put the responsibility for the team in the students' hands—after all, it's their team and their work. If you want to be a state tournament contender in your first year, you'll need some qualified teachers and outside expert help to help coach the students. You might ask the prin-

cipal or the PTA for a slightly higher budget for more materials.
(Science Olympiad, n.d., para. 4–5)

There is a $60 fee to participate in Science Olympiad, but you also will need supplies for some of the challenges.

Like anything, the more experience and familiarity you get, the better your decisions will be. It is difficult to start something if you have not seen it. It might be helpful to find an invitational to attend before you start your team to get a feel for what it looks like. I went to Solon, OH, to see an invitational where there were more than 50 teams competing. Many of the events, such as those involving a test, were closed to the public, but many of the engineering challenges, such as one where an air rocket was launched inside, releasing a ping pong ball with a parachute, were open to all to view. It was explained to me that the longer it took the ping pong ball to reach the ground, the more points a team received. Each event has its own set of rules, so it is important to read up and understand them.

Just like a track meet, there is strategy in who you put in what event. A track coach would want their fastest athletes in the events that involve speed, the strongest for those events that require strength, and the best jumpers for events such as the long jump and hurdles. You will have to determine who is good at the hands-on activities, who knows their stuff and can handle the knowledge-based parts, and who is good at the engineering parts. Developing a team with the necessary components to compete can be a challenge.

Homegrown Idea—STEM Club

What Is This Activity?

A STEM club finds students involved in doing activities that involve the engineering design process (ask, imagine, plan, create, test, improve). The activities can be short-term STEM design challenges that take only a few minutes, to long-term STEM design projects that could take months. No matter which way you choose to go, centering on the design process and reminding students of the process is key. Review more about the engineering design process at https://www.nasa.gov/audience/foreducators/best/edp.html.

Who Can Be Involved?

You can decide which level you want to offer STEM club. I have run STEM clubs at elementary schools, middle schools, and high schools. I probably would not recommend mixing all of these groups together, as students' skills will be at different levels, but I will say I use some of the same challenges with all grade levels. The older students' solutions are simply more complex, but the problems I present involve the same basic premise.

Where Does This Activity Take Place?

I have run all of my clubs in school—some before, some during, and some after—and in a regular classroom. In order to break down the school walls, it is interesting to take students on field trips where they get to see STEM in action in the workplace. I once took a group of students to the Amazon factory where workers use robots to fill orders. The workers explained to us how they used the design process and showed us the robots in action. We also had guest speakers, such as engineering students from the local university, mentor STEM students on some of their long-term projects, providing feedback. The nice thing about running a STEM club is that you do not need any special location to host it. The supplies are all that matters.

When Does This Activity Occur?

Depending on the school, I run my STEM clubs either twice a month or monthly. If you are doing once a month I would recommend doing short-term challenges that would only take that one session. Expecting kids to remember to bring materials or to remember what they were doing after being off for a month is always a challenge. A lot of times I do instant challenges with students based on STEM. You can find many of these online, and there are even demonstrations on YouTube for how to set them up. For instance, here is an instant challenge that I developed called Marshmallow Catapult.

MARSHMALLOW CATAPULT

Materials:
- 10 popsicle sticks
- 3–4 rubber bands
- 1 bottle top
- 1 mini-marshmallow

Build a catapult and see which group can get their marshmallow to go the farthest.

You can even watch a demonstration of the challenge here https://www.youtube.com/watch?v=wTW6QUFtlzQ. This activity's supplies are easy to find, and the catapults are usually super simple to set up. You can have students work by themselves in groups. I alternate on individual activities and small-group tasks depending on the challenge and the materials, but I definitely want students to have the opportunity to work together.

You could do STEM on weekends as a camp. It could be a full day, where by the end, students have used the design process to create a product, such as a video game, a drone, or a bridge, or solve a real-world problem. A full day allows you to spend more focused time with your students without interruption. This would, of course, require you to give up more of your time, although there are some companies that charge students to attend such camps to compensate you.

STEM club does not need to have an end-of-the-year competition, although there are benefits to such a culminating activity. You could host a final instant challenge that involves students putting together the skills they have been working on throughout the year, and invite parents to come watch the process as students create and demonstrate their final products. Again, there are several STEM projects online you could access and use to challenge your students. Another option for an end-of-the-year event would be a showcase during which students demonstrate or exhibit some of the items they have created. I even had students make the showcase interactive, as they demonstrated what they had done and then invited observers to try their hand at creating something themselves.

Why Should Students Participate?

The design process is not just about STEM. This process can be applied to ELA, math, social studies, and life in general. When someone is going to prepare a meal, they go through the design process:

- **Ask:** What do I want for dinner?
- **Imagine:** How many possibilities are there for meals depending on knowledge of how, amount of time you have, as well as materials available?
- **Plan:** Get those materials and make a plan for creating the meal. You can use the backward-building process. If the meal takes 15 minutes to prepare, 30 minutes to cook, and a few minutes to assemble, determine when you want to eat and work backward to know when to start.
- **Create:** Actually put your plan into action, combining materials, preparing them, multitasking multiple dishes, and assembling it all together into one meal.
- **Improve:** Throughout the process you will have opportunities to improve the meal, whether it be something as simple as adding more salt to a hollandaise sauce to improve the overall quality of the meal. There will be plenty of chances to nudge and alter the plan in an attempt to make the meal better.

If students have a really good understanding of the design process, they can use it to their advantage to make what they are working on better.

STEM education has a lot of practical benefits, as laid out by The EdVocate (Lynch, 2019). STEM:

- fosters ingenuity and creativity,
- builds resilience,
- encourages experimentation,
- encourages teamwork,
- encourages knowledge application,
- encourages tech use,
- teaches problem solving, and
- encourages adaption.

I'm sure you see some familiarity with the 21st-century skills discussed earlier in this book.

Even though I don't expressly offer my STEM clubs to just those who have been identified as gifted, when I look at my roster there are a majority of students who are. I think this is because gifted students' curious nature, along with the opportunity to combine their intelligence with their creativity, draws them to such programs like a magnet.

How Do You Run This Activity?

STEM challenges often require providing materials, which can be handled in a couple of ways. You can have the students bring in their own supplies, you can have students bring in general supplies that you add to the cache of materials, you can ask the school to provide you with materials, or there are times when I simply purchased the materials myself. Materials need not be expensive, and some of the best materials to have are very practical. These include:

- toilet/paper towel rolls,
- egg cartons,
- chenille sticks,
- straws,
- coffee filters,
- popsicle sticks,
- index cards,
- rubber bands,
- envelopes, and
- paper clips.

If you are thinking about implementing a STEM club, I have some free projects that I have used with my students to get you started at https://www.thegift edguy.com/resources. I have found these work with all ages of students.

Something Extra to Think About

With innovation and technology driving a lot of our lives in recent years, the introduction of STEM content makes sense because it will help students become the innovators of tomorrow. Don't forget that STEM has always been around. Thomas Edison was using STEM when he worked on the lightbulb, famously experimenting with hundreds of filaments. Cavemen were using STEM the first time one of them thought, "Hey, I wonder if we can use this fire thing for something more practical than just burning stuff down." The point is, STEM is simply another way to look at science. It is merely a way of thinking about things. That is what most of these AECAs involve—thinking about things in different ways, differently than you might typically see in the classroom. Students who think differently stand out and allow the world to continue to advance. We need to be creating more thinkers, not more memorizers.

CHAPTER 5

Social Studies

Social studies is a subject area that is starting to become marginalized. Why? Because social studies in many people's minds is about memorizing names, places, dates, and other facts that can easily be looked up on your phone now. Most of the stuff we learned in social studies class can be answered by Alexa, and therein lies the problem: Why learn something that you can easily look up?

I learned after several years of teaching social studies than content was moot. Although learning historical facts was important, if my students never learned who the Mesopotamians were, this would not prevent them from getting a job. Or, if they forgot who started World War I, they were going to get by in life just fine. My students benefitted the most from learning valuable skills and knowledge related to citizenship, public speaking, leadership, government, economics, and global awareness. These are all skills that are required to be successful in life, and so having opportunities in which students can learn these is extremely important. The great thing about AECAs involving social studies is that students are able to put these skills into action, using authentic situations to develop their abilities.

National Speech and Debate Association

What Is This Activity?

The National Speech and Debate Association (NSDA; https://www.speech anddebate.org) outlines a variety of competition events on its website. Speech and debate can help students master a variety of skills, including crucial 21st-century skills, such as creativity, persuasion, collaboration, adaptability, and emotional intelligence (NSDA, n.d.-b).

Speech is a presentation by either individual students or a group, and students' performance is compared to that of other students giving similar speeches. The competitions range from speeches that require impromptu interpretations to extensively researched speech events. NSDA outlines 16 events in the speech category divided between high school and middle school, including commentary, dramatic interpretation, humorous interpretation, and informative speaking (see https://www.speechanddebate.org/competition-events for the complete list). The debate events involve an individual or team of debaters whose goal is to convince the judges that their argument is more valid than that of the opposing team. The events can include congressional debates, policy debates, public forum debates, and Lincoln-Douglas debates. Students can compete individually and win awards based on their specific category. If you have a larger number of students, they can act as a team. Students will compete in individual events but be given a team score based on how all of your students perform.

Students can try a few categories and can change their category from invitational to invitational; however, if they are to get really good at one category, it would make sense to build skills in one area. Typically, students either choose speech or debate, and they do not participate in both at the same tournament, as this presents a scheduling issue.

Who Can Be Involved?

NSDA outlines event options for both middle and high school students. The speech category has specific events for each grade-level band. Here is an example of a difference between those levels:

- **Commentary (High School):** Students are presented with prompts related to societal, political, historic or popular culture and, in 20 minutes, prepare a five-minute speech responding to the prompt. Students may consult articles and evidence they gather prior to the contest, but may not use the internet during preparation. The speech is delivered from memory and no notes are allowed.
- **Declamation (Middle School):** Students bring history to life—literally—by delivering a speech that has been delivered by someone else. From the historical greats to contemporary public orations, students have 10 minutes to perform a memorized speech with an introduction. Topics can vary widely based on the interest of the student. The goal of Declamation is for the student to perform another speaker's message in their own voice. (NSDA, n.d.-a)

Some of the categories have very specific formats that must be followed, while others are more loosely structured.

Where Does This Activity Take Place?

The journey for speech and debate begins at the local school level with students learning what a good speech and/or debate looks like. Students try various formats, such as the Lincoln-Douglas, cross-examination, and others. In most states there are local opportunities to experience each of these competition categories throughout the school year in order to practice their formats and gain confidence in using them at invitationals. At one tournament the students might give an expository speech. At another they might give a dramatic interpretation. These events are usually publicized on the state website for speech and debate. Much like a sports team, a speech and debate team can travel to different venues each week to compete against others and develop skills.

These invitational meets lead up to the district tournament in which students compete in the various categories, with those who score the highest qualifying for the state tournament. Then, the best teams from each district square off at the state tournament. This can be a 1–2-day event depending on the state. Your best bet for knowing which of these schedules your state uses is to check your state's website for speech and debate (see https://www.speechanddebate. org/partnerships/#state-orgs for a list by state). The judges' decisions will determine who moves on to the National Tournament (see https://www.speechand debate.org/nationals).

The National Tournament has speech and debate activities for more than 140,000 students from around the country to participate in. There are college scholarships at stake for the top competitors. Students are judged by CEOs, former cabinet members, stage and screen celebrities, and acclaimed community members.

When Does This Activity Occur?

Invitationals take place in the months leading up to the district tournament, commonly from October to January. Teams may travel every weekend, gaining experience at each event. Students usually have to go to a certain number of invitationals in order to be able to participate in the district tournament. These district tournaments are spread throughout the state depending on the size of the state and the number of participants. These can take place anywhere from mid-December to late January. The state tournament is about a month after the district tournaments. The middle school and high school national tournaments overlap with one another during the summer months.

Why Should Students Participate?

Public speaking is a highly valued 21st-century skill. It gives students an advantage over others who are not as comfortable with public speaking. It also requires students to be prepared to argue both sides of the issue, meaning they become more open-minded. By competing in speech and debate, students will:

- build their public speaking tools with resources and other training tools,
- develop communication skills that are valued by employers, and
- learn to analyze problems, discuss and debate them in a civil manner, and collaborate together to create solutions.

Although learning how to publicly speak is great for all students, it is really a good format for gifted students who need to find their voice. I have taught most grade levels of students, and I can always quickly tell who the gifted students are at the elementary level because they are the most outspoken, have something to share, and aren't afraid to give their opinion. As these gifted students get older, they can become more and more difficult to identify because they learn not only social graces, but also that others have come to resent their "know-it-all" status. As a result, they learn to better "fit in" by being quieter, but this results in them not able to express themselves as fully as they can. Instead of suppressing gifted students' voices, we need to find avenues where they can use them. Avenues of public speaking, such as speech and debate, are excellent conduits and also allow gifted students to use their higher level thinking skills.

How Do You Run This Activity?

First and foremost, the team advisor has to work with the district to make sure tournaments are paid for or to ask permission to raise funds. Depending on how many invitationals a team attends, there is also the added cost of transporting students to these tournaments. The advisor also has to raise interest in the team if one has not already been established. This means educating students on what is involved in participating.

The National Speech and Debate website has all sorts of tools to help you to prepare your team (see https://www.speechanddebate.org/store), such as books outlining the debate formats, videos of competitors at the National Tournament, and resources for questions that can be used at your invitational tournaments or practices.

Regardless of the tools you use, the general idea is that you will be showing students how to properly make an argument within a structure. You can start students out with speeches and debates on more "fun" topics, such as whether college athletes should be paid or not or whether the chicken or the egg came first. These informal speeches and debates will generate excitement. You can work up to speeches and debates that have time limits and particular structures, elements students will see while participating in this competition.

You also might have to teach students how to conduct proper research and how to use that information to strengthen an argument. You could have discussions on what compelling evidence looks like and why some information might be more pertinent than other facts to include. Much like writing an essay, a speech or debate states a thesis, and all that follows should support a student's argument.

Mock Trial

What Is This Activity?

Mock trial involves teams of students preparing for a trial and then arguing a case against other teams. Taking part in mock trial can provide students with valuable skills and give them a taste of the real-world experiences of attorneys and the nation's legal system.

Who Can Be Involved?

Mock trial can be used at the elementary level, middle school level, and high school level. Elementary and middle school students might present fictional mock trials based on fairy tales or other stories (see Blauvelt & Cote, 2012, as an example) at the classroom or school level. There are no national competitions at the elementary and middle school levels. In some states, there are state-level competition opportunities at the middle school level. In Ohio, for example, the cases are based on popular books. These middle school competitions have based trials on the books *Holes*, *Lord of the Flies*, and *The Giver*, just to name a few. Sometimes the middle school opportunities are not competitions, but rather showcases for students to be able to show their skills. In other cases, middle school competitions involve more real-world cases and follow much the same rules as high school competitions with less emphasis on some rules. You may need to research what competitions are available in your state or considerations for building your own school-level mock trial competition.

At the high school level, the cases are very much real-world experiences. The competitions are structured just like actual courtroom proceedings. The competition culminates in the annual National High School Mock Trial Championship (https://www.nationalmocktrial.org). High schools form teams with about 11 students on the roster, with 6–9 official members (National High School Mock Trial Championship, 2020). Some schools have multiple teams. Teams should ideally include two defense attorneys, two defense witnesses, two prosecuting attorneys, two prosecution witnesses, one bailiff/time keeper, and two alternates.

Each team must prepare for both sides of the case they are presented with. A team will face two opponents during the mock trial. Half of the team represents the prosecution in the case that students have prepared for and squares off against another school's team. Meanwhile, the other half of the team acts as the defense and goes up against a different team. In the courtroom, teams follow the same order as an actual trial (i.e., prosecution's opening statement, defense's opening statement, examination of prosecution and defense witnesses, and closing statements from both sides). There is no jury present, but three judges evaluate how effective the argument is as well as the performances of the witnesses. There is also a time limit for each of the actions. Opening and closing statements get 5 minutes per side, and the examination and cross-examinations are allotted about 20 minutes per side (National High School Mock Trial Championship, 2020).

Where Does This Activity Take Place?

To make the experience as authentic as possible, most mock trials are held in actual courtrooms. At the high school level, district competitions are usually held at a local courthouse. Regionals expand this area a bit more to find a venue that is appropriate. State competitions are typically held in a major city of the state, utilizing its courthouse. The National High School Mock Trial Championship rotates amongst various cities. The past few years it has been hosted in cities like Athens, GA, Reno, NV, and Hartford, CT. You could easily host a school-level competition for your classroom, or for several classrooms, at any grade level.

When Does This Activity Occur?

At the high school level, students receive their packets with their case in September. Each packet provides an overview of the case and profiles for the possible witnesses, as well as exhibits that can be used in court as evidence. Students work on preparing this case over the next couple of months, determining who will best fill each role in the courtroom.

Teams typically have a scrimmage or two prior to the district tournament, so that they get a feel for the actual competition. Then, in January the district competitions occur, with those teams who win both their prosecution and their defense case moving on to regionals in February. If you win both sides of your case here, your team goes to the state competition in March. At all of these levels of competition, there are awards for best lawyers as well as best witnesses.

In the end, each state sends a single team to the National High School Mock Trial Championship. Each state has to pay a membership fee of $250, and the team has a tournament registration fee of $500. There is a new case released at the beginning of April in order to give teams a month to prepare. The National Championship is held traditionally over Mother's Day weekend (first week or so in May), with the proceedings lasting from Wednesday to Sunday, with teams taking part in scrimmages early in the week and picking up their scores Sunday morning.

Why Should Students Participate?

Mock trial lets students see the legal system in action. There are lot of things students learn in social studies class that they will never have to know again. However, having a good understanding of how our legal system works will benefit most everyone because at one point or another, students will find themselves dealing with it, whether it be something as extreme as a criminal case, as benign as a civil suit, or as common as a will or a marriage.

In addition, mock trial is good training for a possible career in law. Many participants who take part in mock trial develop a love for law and pursue careers as lawyers. What better way to prepare students for such an endeavor than to let them experience what it would be like firsthand?

Mock trial provide students with opportunities to build public speaking skills much like speech and debate, but also adds a certain improvisational element where students have to think quickly on their feet when examining an opponent's witness, or have to shift the argument in reaction to something the other side does in the courtroom. This adaptability requires gifted students to use their critical thinking skills and problem solve in an authentic situation.

How Do You Run This Activity?

An advisor for mock trial does not have to have a lot of experience with courtroom proceedings and law. Many times, they organize the team and assign parts, but the specifics of the case and arguments of the lawyers will be shaped by the legal advisor for the team. This is typically a lawyer who is willing to give up their time to advise the team and share their own legal expertise. If you find a good legal advisor, they will do most of the heavy lifting in preparing the team for the courtroom.

There are some districts that run mock trial as an afterschool program during which students try out for the team. Other schools run it as a class during which the team is selected from the best performers or multiple teams are formed. Sometimes the timing of your club depends upon the legal advisor your team has. If the legal advisor is available during the day, you could run it as a class. If, however, the legal advisor is only available after regular working hours, you might have to have practices later in the day to accommodate this.

There are lots of cases available that can be used to help students gain an understanding of mock trial. Many states release past cases, which you can download for free from their sites. The National High School Mock Trial Championship also has a repository of old cases that are available to state coordinators in the members area of the website.

National Geographic GeoBee

What Is This Activity?

National Geographic sponsors a geography bee every year for middle school students (https://www.nationalgeographic.org/education/student-experiences/geobee). It is designed to see how knowledgeable students are about the world around them, not just where things are located, but what sorts of animals live where, the habitats, and the culture.

Who Can Be Involved?

The GeoBee is for grades 4–8. Students may not sign up for the GeoBee individually, but rather must be a representative of a school that has registered with National Geographic. In order for a school to participate, there must be at least six students competing. Advisors can register at the website at https://geobee-registration.nationalgeographic.com. As of 2020, the competition costs $120 per school. You could have several schools within a district participating in GeoBee; however, each one would need to register and pay the fee. If you had three middle schools in your district, each one could hold its own GeoBee and name a champion. Then each of the winners would get the chance to qualify for the state championship through the online portion of the competition.

Where Does This Activity Take Place?

The GeoBee has three different levels students can compete at. It starts at the school level. Individual schools crown GeoBee champions who are eligible to qualify for the state level. There are various ways these school champions can be determined. Some examples National Geographic suggests include:

- Conduct an oral competition in each classroom, determine each classroom's winner (or top two if you have less than 10 classrooms), and then hold a final competition with up to 10 students.
- For a smaller group of students, conduct an oral competition for the preliminary and final rounds at the same time. Remember the final round can only have up to 10 students.
- Conduct a written preliminary competition using the written test provided in the school GeoBee materials, and hold an oral final round competition with up to 10 students. (National Geographic, n.d., Participation/Format, sec. 9)

Regardless of how the school chooses to conduct the school level competition, after deciding who will represent the school, the advisor is provided with a login and a testing window that must be used to take the online state qualifying test. This online test is monitored by the GeoBee coordinator and must be taken in school. Once the test is started, students have only 60 minutes to take the test. The deadline for this testing window is usually the first week in February. The top 100 students from the state are then invited to represent their school at the State GeoBee, usually held around the end of March.

At the state competition, students go through eight rounds of questions, each correct answer scoring the student a point. The various rounds are:

- cultural geography;
- economic geography;
- across-the-country, around-the-world;
- science;
- geographic comparisons;
- physical geography; and
- odd-item-out (a category where one contestant is given three choices, plus a description and chooses the one that doesn't fit).

The top 10 students then go into the final round and are eliminated if they answer two questions incorrectly. Once two contestants remain, the competition enters the championship round, during which there are three questions asked of both participants. The student who correctly answers the most questions is the state champion. The winner receives an all-expenses paid trip to Washington, DC, to be the state representative at the National GeoBee Championship.

When Does This Activity Occur?

The GeoBee occurs throughout the school year, with the national championship usually occurring in May. The National Geographic website will have valuable updates about each year's competition schedule: https://www.nationalgeographic.org/education/student-experiences/geobee.

Why Should Students Participate?

Today we can all rely on smartphones to determine where we are and where to go, so it might seem like geography is not as important a subject area as it once was. Geography, of course, goes far beyond knowing where a location is. Students learn about culture, science, physical features of the Earth and the atmosphere, economics, population and resource distribution, land use, and more. They begin to understand larger global connections, including how where you live has a great influence on how you live, how human activity affects the world, and more. GeoBee also employs students' research and critical thinking skills, as they study and prepare for the competition.

How Do You Run This Activity?

After registering your school and paying the fee, the first thing you need to do is form a group of students who will participate in the GeoBee. This can be done by interest, by teacher recommendation, by having students take a preliminary test to qualify, or with an entire class. Depending on when you are holding your GeoBee, you will have a good amount of time to figure out who would like to participate, including which students have stronger geography skills and background, in order to make it manageable for the Bee. You likely do not want to have more than 30 students taking part in the GeoBee.

Most of the tools provided by National Geographic can be found at https://www.nationalgeographic.org/education/student-experiences/geobee/study. There is also a rich number of lesson plans National Geographic provides for teachers to use for geography. These can be accessed at https://www.nationalgeographic.org/education/student-experiences/geobee/study/study-resources.

Then it is a matter of organizing the GeoBee. Getting a couple of teachers or parents to help judge would be helpful. Much like a spelling bee, you can invite family and friends to watch the competition. With your registration fee, National Geographic provides all of the questions you will use for the three rounds of the Bee as well as a medal for the winner. Once the Bee is over, you can provide the time and space for the winner to take their online test to qualify for the state tournament and then check to see if they scored in the top 100.

Model United Nations

What Is This Activity?

Model United Nations deals with diplomacy, international relations, and global perspective. Different states and countries run Model UN differently, but the general idea is that students act as representatives for a specific country. As representatives of this country, they become experts on its culture and government, and use this knowledge to either negotiate with other nations or plead to the United Nations for help with a problem plaguing their country.

Keep in mind that there might be several organizations that sponsor within your state, each with a different way of doing things. For example, some organizations choose the topics prior to the conference, and students research and prepare a position their country is going to have on the topic. Others might involve students choosing the topic beforehand and writing how they plan to solve a problem happening in their country. Yet another organization might run the competition and have students show up for the event before receiving their scenario, requiring teams to develop their strategies on the spot.

Who Can Be Involved?

Model UN is for high school students, but many states also have a program for middle schoolers (grades 6–8). For example, Ohio hosts Junior Ohio Model United Nations. There are also some universities that sponsor Model UN teams at the collegiate level.

Where Does This Activity Take Place?

The location depends on who is running the Model UN. Some are large conferences held in places such as New York City and Washington, DC, and others are more local. There are also several different entities who offer Model UN. For example, in Ohio, there is Model UN sponsored by the YMCA and OMUN run by the Ohio Leadership Institute. Some Model UN competitions are held at universities, such as the Ohio State University High School Model United Nations conference, while organizations such as Cleveland Council on World Affairs sponsor a Model UN conference for middle and high schoolers. Your best bet for finding out where Model UN takes place in your city or state is to do an online search to see what the offerings are.

When Does This Activity Occur?

Timing depends on which organization is running the event you are participating in. The Model United Nations at the University of Chicago (https://munuc.org) is considered one of the largest conferences in the world and is held in the early spring. Every year National Model United Nations (https://www.nmun.org), in the spirit of international diplomacy, holds its conference across the globe. For example, the conferences in 2021 are anticipated to be held in

New York in April, and Washington, DC, Kobe, Japan, and Olomouc, Czech Republic, in November 2021. If there is a certain time of the year that would be better than others to take students, you could find a Model UN nearby to attend that fits your schedule.

Why Should Students Participate?

As a social studies teacher, Model UN is one way I could teach my students global awareness. It is one thing to read about global awareness in a book or be asked about it on a test. With Model UN, I felt that students were getting to have an authentic experience. Although the experience may not be as authentic as being at the actual United Nations and working with people from all over the world, it allows students to role-play and to collaborate with others who might think differently than they do. Even though it was a localized version of cultural immersion, with students from all over the state, listening to students talk about issues they are passionate about and learning about problems others in the world face cause students to have a more well-rounded perspective and understanding of the world.

There are, of course, the 21st-century skills students acquire as well. Public speaking would be first and foremost, as students must defend their positions as well as argue against positions they do not agree with. Students must research to learn about their country and to be able to make a viable argument for why their position is a legitimate one. This falls under accessing and analyzing information. Adaptation is an important skill to possess, given that as much as students prepare their arguments, in the end they do not know the opposing arguments that may emerge, which means they have to adapt to the arguments as they come. Problem solving is certainly used, as that is what Model UN is all about—solving the world's problems. What I always find interesting about Model UN is the originality and ingenuity of how students tackle the issues they are presented with. For example, Eritrea might have an issue with consistent power for the citizens of its country as well as an overreliance on fossil fuels, but it is also terribly confined to limited land available. A creative solution might be to install floating solar panels in the ocean that do not take away space on land, and provide more clean and consistent power. Another problem might involve an island nation that is experiencing the destruction of its coral reef. Students might research a solution that involves placing stone statues in the ocean that prevent destruction from happening and suggest soliciting donors to pay for them if the statues are in their form.

Finally, students build their collaboration skills, as they must work together not only with the people from their own country in order to develop their positions, but also with others as they network and convince others of their arguments. This can be a valuable skill for gifted students to develop, because some of them do not work well in groups. It can be a variety of reasons, such as not suffering fools gladly, feeling like they have to do all of the work themselves, believing they know better than others, or having learned to work independently over the years. The skill of collaboration is not saying the best argument, but rather listening to someone else who might have a better one. It involves compromise, which can be tough for some students, as well as a willingness to build on ideas together. Groups should be able to produce something better through their collective efforts than any one individual could. Learning this lesson is a valuable life skill in appreciating why we work with others.

How Do You Run This Activity?

I have run Model UN both as a part of my classroom curriculum and as a before- or afterschool club. When I taught it as part of my curriculum, it was easy to tie it to some of the standards I was required to teach, such as culture, geography, public speaking, research, and group work. My students and I spent a lot of time talking about what a good argument looked like, how to make that argument, and how to improve the argument. In addition, I assigned students one of these ambassador roles:

- Ambassador of Foreign Relations
- Ambassador of Economics
- Ambassador of Culture
- Ambassador of History
- Ambassador of Politics

Students spent a couple of weeks researching certain aspects of their country, which meant they had to become the expert on their topic. For instance, the ambassador of foreign relations needs to learn the following information:

1. Which nations share a border or are close by your nation?
2. What is the relationship with most of these countries, and how does it affect the region?
3. Who is your county's biggest ally, and why? Who would be considered its biggest enemy?
4. Has your country been involved in any wars in the last 100 years, and if so, with or against what other countries?
5. What is the land type? Describe the land features of your nation, such as mountains, rivers, deserts, etc.
6. Describe the climate of your nation. How much rainfall does your nation receive annually?

7. Do any of the geographic features of your nation cause problems or create situations of great concern?
8. Describe any unique geographic features of your nation. Do any geographic features divide the people of your nation, ethnically or culturally?

By each of the group members becoming an expert on their topic, groups could jigsaw together whatever they needed to make their argument and be able to answer any challenges to their position paper.

I have lately been running Model UN as a before-school and afterschool club. Because there is not the time afforded to me in the classroom, the focus becomes teaching the students the proper procedures and formatting their argument must take. We spend some time practicing the speeches and adjusting the arguments, but there is also getting the parent permission forms, registering them with Model UN, getting their position papers in, and other clerical work that is needed for students to participate. I feel that the experience of meeting with students from all over the state, all with different views and perspectives, offers students the chance to learn not only about global awareness, but also about their own community.

Homegrown Idea—Cultural Appreciation Club

What Is This Activity?

Cultural appreciation clubs involve students celebrating the diversity of other cultures and other points of view. There are various reasons for forming cultural appreciation clubs. Your school might have a large population of a certain culture and thus want to celebrate it. You may want to celebrate diversity and multiculturalism in general. You could also promote language learning and cultural awareness through Spanish Club or Chinese Club. You, yourself, may have a specific passion for a particular culture or country. You can also celebrate and build understanding of underrepresented groups through an African American Club, a Women's Club, or a LGBTQ Club.

However you decide to run the club, it is important that you have individuals who feel passionately about the studied culture, that you develop a forum to be able to educate others about it, and that you have a goal or project in mind that the club can work toward.

Who Can Be Involved?

Although you can start a cultural appreciation club for various reasons, most are built organically by a group of students who feel very strongly about a specific cultural group. You can begin such a group at any level of schooling.

Where Does This Activity Take Place?

No matter how you decide to run the actual club, you should make sure to have a showcase or project in mind that will allow your students to demonstrate aspects of the culture and teach others about it. This could be something as simple as having a potluck of cultural dishes and inviting the school and/or public to try these dishes and learn about their history, as well as more about the culture in general. This could involve having a school assembly where the culture is portrayed, such as a Black History Month program where that culture is celebrated through the reading of poetry, performing of music, and reenactments of famous and critical moments in Black history. You could host a Community Festival where you showcase many of the different cultures that exist in your school district. Our district had a CommUNITY Festival where students performed dances from their home countries, gave fashion shows, provided various arts and crafts from around the world, as well as many other activities for people to participate in. Again, the main idea of a cultural appreciation club is to educate others about the culture(s). That is why it is important to find a venue or project through which the culture can be showcased effectively and reach the greatest number of people.

When Does This Activity Occur?

Cultural appreciation clubs will vary in how they are run, depending on the focus. For example, if the goal of the club is to provide an education program honoring Dr. Martin Luther King, Jr., the preparation would need to be done by January. If the goal is to have a beginning-of-the-year celebration to show how diverse the school district is, then you might have to start planning the year before. There can be several end-of-the-year celebrations that would take place in May or June. You may have a celebration coincide with a very special time of year. For example, for Islamic History Club, you might want to use Ramadan to create awareness of the culture, letting non-Islamic students experience what it is like to fast and learning about why it is practiced, or inviting them to Eid al-Fitr, which is the celebration at the end of the month.

The club should start with the end goal in mind and work backward from there. You might need an entire school year and meet once a month with students. You might only need a couple of months where you meet every week. You might meet every day over a couple of weeks. The end goal will dictate the needs of the group.

Why Should Students Participate?

Understanding different cultures is a major part of building students' global awareness. One of my teachers used to say that, "There are approximately 350,000 births every day, and on this day, those babies are more like one another than they will ever be the rest of their lives." This always resonated with me because the biggest difference between me and a person halfway across the globe is our culture. Culture is what makes us different, which is great, but the lack of understanding of a culture can cause a lot of problems. That is why cultural appreciation clubs are so valuable because they do two things: (1) They allow students to celebrate their culture, understand other cultures, and be proud of their identity, and (2) they allow students to educate others about cultural differences and history.

How Do You Run This Activity?

Running a cultural club, of course, is going to depend on the age range of the students in the club, as well as its focus. The important thing is that you give as many opportunities as possible for members to either share their culture or to learn about the culture of the group they are studying. This might be watching films that represent that culture well, such as *Coco* for elementary/middle school students to show Mexican culture, or *Roma* for older students. This could involve bringing in members of that culture to share with the group, whether it is in a Q&A, an interview, or through another format, such as if there is something specific about their culture they would like to share like a holiday or ever-popular food.

Be careful to make sure that students do not represent the culture as a stereotype. Culture clubs do need to be run with a level of sensitivity and with a message of inclusivity and tolerance.

Something Extra to Think About

The ultimate goal of social studies is to create well-rounded global citizens who want to make the vast world around them a little smaller by learning about things heretofore unfamiliar to them. Most of the AECAs in this chapter take students out their classroom bubble and expose them to authentic experiences. Because the situations are authentic, students see how the real world works beyond the classroom and the value in learning tolerance and an understanding of cultures that are different than their own. Such valuable life lessons show why social studies should not be marginalized as a subject area and how important a role it will play in students' lives.

CHAPTER **6**

Leadership

Leadership is one of those skills that everyone agrees is valuable, but not a lot of people know how to teach it explicitly. There are not many content standards that focus on this skill, there are not often classes aimed at teaching leadership, and there is usually no test at the end of the year to determine who has learned leadership or not. And yet who wouldn't want students to be skilled leaders? For that matter, who wouldn't want a potential employee who displays good leadership skills?

Leadership is often taught in our extracurricular activities, mostly sports. More often than not, athletes who can lead their teams successfully will have more victories than those without a leader. Leadership comes naturally from the sport itself, and students who are successful are those who make themselves someone others want to follow. The same goes for academic extracurricular activities. Because many of the competitions have a team aspect to them, having a leader on this team is crucial to its success. Without that leader, the group wanders aimlessly and is not able to accom-

DOI: 10.4324/9781003234982-7

plish what it needs. There are some AECAs that explicitly develop leadership skills, such as:

- active listening,
- reliability,
- dependability,
- positivity,
- effective feedback,
- timely communication,
- team building,
- flexibility,
- risk-taking, and
- mentorship.

Students participating in these activities will learn skills such as these through intellectually challenging activities, which will make these students even more valuable to employers.

It is important that gifted students learn what leadership looks like. The National Association for Gifted Children stated the following on its website:

> Some gifted children may be perceived as bossy or domineering, when they are enthusiastic about a new idea or invention. They may be so intensely involved they don't notice the other children's reactions or lack of interest. Gifted children can learn the difference between leadership and bossiness.
>
> Some tips for helping your child navigate the nuances:
> - Help them understand that a good leader lets others have ideas and input and doesn't always make all the decisions
> - Share with them the aspects of leadership—delegating, assisting, helping, facilitating
> - Talk about the differences between bossiness and cooperation
> - Provide outlets for leadership skills to emerge, either at home or within the community (Webb et al., 2007, as cited in National Association for Gifted Children, n.d.)

These AECAs provide just such an outlet for gifted students to learn about leadership and to hone their skills.

DECA

What Is This Activity?

DECA (https://www.deca.org) was first formed as a way to connect students who worked a vocation with the school. Clubs were created under the premise that these students could learn valuable marketing skills without having to leave the school building. DECA has evolved along with the latest technology and changes in business practices. The main goal of DECA is to prepare students to become leaders in career fields, such as marketing, finance, hospitality, and management, by putting them in as many real-life situations as possible. DECA is usually offered as part of a class, but the extracurricular aspect has to do with the competition series DECA provides to give students opportunities to take vocational skills that they have learned and apply them to realistic scenarios.

The competitive events fall into six different career clusters:
- business management and administration,
- entrepreneurship,
- marketing,
- finance,
- hospitality and tourism, and
- personal financial literacy.

Who Can Be Involved?

DECA is primarily for high school students, although one of the nice things is that participants can carry it on into college, as 275 colleges have a DECA chapter. In order to be able to take part in the competition in high school, a student has to be enrolled in an approved course that usually is in business, marketing, finance, hospitality, or entrepreneurship taught by a qualified instructor who becomes the advisor. Not every school has one of these classes, but many do. Typically, in this class students are introduced to the business principals they will be using in the competition. Students then pick a specific event from the list of 10 they would like to participate in and prepare for that. The event categories are (DECA, n.d.):
- Principles of Business Administration,
- Team Decision Making,
- Individual Series,
- Personal Finance Literacy,
- Business Operations Research,
- Project Management,

- Entrepreneurship,
- Marketing Representative,
- Professional Selling and Consulting, and
- Online.

Some events are written, some are presentations, and some combine both, while others are only online. Complete descriptions of all of the events can be found at https://www.deca.org/high-school-programs/high-school-competitive-events.

Sometimes classes take part in school-based enterprises that involve opening a business. This could be something a small as selling T-shirts or candy bars, to operating the school store. This provides some students with their first work experience and allows them to see firsthand how businesses can operate.

Where Does This Activity Take Place?

The DECA competition has three levels to it. The first of these is the district competition. Each state has divided up the territories into regions, and each one of these hosts a district tournament. Georgia, where DECA enrollment is fairly large, has 10 districts. Each one of these regions holds a district tournament at a high school in the area, with some regions holding two tournaments depending on their size.

From the district-level competitions, students qualify for the state competition, which takes part at the State Career Development Conference. This is typically a 2-day event where students compete against the best in the state. If students perform well, they will be invited to the International Career Development Conference (ICDC). There, students will continue to compete in the events they have participated in, and for other attendees there is an emerging leader series where students can work on 21st-century skills, such as communication, critical thinking, collaborating with others, and creativity. Beyond the ICDC, DECA also sponsors an Emerging Leader Summit in July, as well as regional leadership conferences in November.

When Does This Activity Occur?

The district tournaments usually take place in December or January. The State Career Development Conference is set by each state, but each state's usually takes place within the window of late February to mid-March.

The International Career Development Conference moves from year to year. This is held toward the end of April in various cities, such as Atlanta, GA,

Orlando, FL, and Anaheim, CA. For a most recent list of cities and their dates, you can visit https://www.deca.org/high-school-programs/high-school-education al-conferences/international-career-development-conference-hs.

Why Should Students Participate?

As Chapter 2 discussed, learning 21st-century skills is very important. Learning how they work in the real world and getting the opportunity to use them in an authentic situation makes the skills even more valuable. DECA focuses on developing students who will be leaders in the business community. There is a specific leadership aspect to DECA that students can grow by taking part in the DECA class, competing in the DECA events, and attending the DECA leadership conferences. To foster this, there are opportunities to run for office and put these leadership skills into play while helping to run and advise the organization.

How Do You Run This Activity?

Compared to many of the programs in this book, DECA has two large differences. One is that, in order to be a DECA advisor, you have to be a career/ technical educator. This means not just anyone can run a DECA classroom. The advisor has to be approved by the state as a degreed teacher with completion of coursework or work experience in career/tech. The other difference is that DECA is not usually run as a before-school or afterschool club. Rather, it is considered cocurricular, which means it is taught within the confines of the school day and scheduled as a class.

There is a comprehensive advisor handbook that can be accessed at https:// www.deca.org/wp-content/uploads/2019/09/2019_Advisor_Guidebook.pdf. It even provides you with a monthly calendar to keep your timeline going and offers ideas for activities. For example, here is a sample schedule for January:

- Ask business professionals to help your members prepare for competitive events.
- Make plans to attend your association's career development conference.
- Participate in DECA's online events and activities.
- Polish and submit student scholarship applications.
- Recruit members who have joined your class during the second semester.
- Submit DECA Emerging Leader Honor Award applications. (DECA, 2019, p. 15)

Key Club

What Is This Activity?

Key Club (https://www.keyclub.org) provides opportunities for students to volunteer in their community or elsewhere in order to help others. Key Club is service learning at its finest. It is a kids' branch of the Kiwanis International, which is an organization for adults to better their community both local and abroad with service projects.

Projects the club undertakes can be something as small as picking up trash at the local park, to much larger initiatives, such as helping others in a foreign country who have been hit by an earthquake by raising donations, collecting food items, or creating earthquake kits and sending them overseas. Key Club chapters pick both short- and long-term service projects to work on and then devote their efforts to fulfilling their goals.

Common service projects a Key Club might work on include:
- Send a kid to summer camp.
- Organize a drive for supplies for animal shelters.
- Beautify parks in your neighborhood.
- Pledge to a family.
- Start a recycling effort.
- Work with Meals on Wheels.
- Organize a blood drive.
- Donate your old phones.
- Collect sports equipment for kids.
- Raise awareness.

Who Can Be Involved?

Key Clubs are usually formed in high schools, but there are some community-based ones not run by the school. Students must be willing to serve at least 50 hours of community service in order to maintain membership.

There are elected officers such as president, vice president(s), secretary, treasurer, and directors from each grade level, which require students to be leaders. Students then decide as an organization what service projects they are going to undertake. Many districts will have an overarching service project. If students really enjoy Key Club, they have the option of joining the Kiwanis when they get older. In addition to other activities, the Key Club could take on the Kiwanis mission, which of late has been eliminating the risk of maternal/neonatal tetanus in countries all over the world.

Where Does This Activity Take Place?

There are Key Club chapters on every continent except Antarctica. There are 33 organized districts in the United States. Each of these districts is led by a student governor who is elected at the annual district convention.

The actual service learning might happen all around the community. The service project could be students running a car wash and then putting the proceeds toward a social issue. It could be students volunteering at the senior center by reading to elderly people or playing games. It might be students hosting a trick-or-treat event for children in their neighborhood. But this reach can extend beyond the immediate community. The service project could be students writing get-well cards and sending them to children in Korea, fighting a river disease in Africa, or selling Yuda Bands to fund educational initiatives in Guatemala.

There are various types of conferences. Each district conducts its own, and there is also the possibility of attending an international conference. By accessing https://www.keyclub.org/district-information-conventions, you find out where and when the conference is going to be held for your area. The international conference moves from year to year to provide access to different chapters from around the country. The last few conventions have been held in cities like San Francisco, CA, Chicago, IL, and San Antonio, TX.

When Does This Activity Occur?

Beyond regular club meetings, Key Clubs participate in special events throughout the year (Kiwanis International, 2017). Key Club Week is during the first week of November to "promote the service Key Clubbers do within their homes, schools and communities" (p. 48). Each district hosts a convention in the spring, which includes election of district offers, training of club officers, and awards for dedicated clubs. Most of these are 2-day conferences held between mid-March and early April. Kiwanis One Day is the first Saturday and April and is billed as a united day of service for Key Clubs and Kiwanis clubs. And, at the International Conference, which is in the summer usually at the beginning of July, students have the opportunity to gather with clubs from around the world to learn about new programs, earn awards, attend workshops, and elect international officers.

Why Should Students Participate?

Leadership is one of the most fundamental skills that is taught through Key Club, as it is student led. Students have the autonomy to decide what they are going to do and then make it happen. They elect officers to help lead. Another benefit is that studies show that students who spend time serving others tend to do better in school. The Key Club follows a formula for building service leadership: Heart to Serve + Call to Lead + Courage to Engage = Service Leadership (Kiwanis International, 2017, p. 17). The goal is to create citizens who want to do the right thing for their community and help others. Most high school students want to do something to help their community. The Key Club just provides them with a forum and structure to do so.

How Do You Run This Activity?

There are some basic requirements in order to be able to begin a chapter of Key Club at your school, including receiving principal support following club membership rules. The cost for students to participate in Key Club is around $10–$14 per student. This purchases both their district membership as well as the international one. There is an advisor packet that you can use to guide your chapter. See https://www.keyclub.org/resources/advisor-guide/guide_faculty_kiwanis-advisor-guide. Additional responsibilities of the Key Club advisor include the following:

- Ensure the Key Club meets regularly—ideally, once a week.
- Oversee that the club follows both international and district bylaws of Key Club.
- Encourage club members to stand up and express their ideas and opinions.
- Assist in sending club members to district and Key Club International conventions.
- Work with the club secretary and treasurer to pay dues to Key Club International and the district in a timely manner and confirm that all members who have paid dues have been entered in the Membership Update Center and are active on the club's roster. (Kiwanis International, 2017, p. 13)

Youth and Government

What Is This Activity?

Youth and Government (http://www.ymcayag.org) is a program run through the local YMCA through which students get to practice democracy. Students write bills and then argue for their passage amongst their fellow students. As a bonus, they typically get to do this in the very place their state legislators do this very thing for real, debating their bills on the floor of the statehouse. This is a great program for anyone who is interested in politics and civics, or who is very passionate about a particular topic. Youth and Government puts leadership and citizenship into action.

Who Can Be Involved?

Youth and Government is designed for students grades 6–12. Students do not necessarily have to be interested in politics in order to participate. If students feel very strongly about a particular issue, such as autism, social work, or gun violence in schools, Youth and Government can act as a platform for them to express their voice and be heard. This program teaches students to be advocates for issues they feel are important and about the system they must use in order to make changes. It teaches them how to be active and good citizens.

Youth and Government also is run by the students, so leadership is encouraged because every year candidates run for offices for the following year. These offices include governor, cabinet members, speaker of the house, or other positions. Students give speeches and campaign for their positions much like real-world politicians would.

Where Does This Activity Take Place?

Currently, Youth and Government takes place in 38 states, as well as Washington, DC. Most states make an effort to host the introduction and arguing of bills at the statehouse. This adds to the authenticity of the program because students sit in the very seats and argue on the very floors that their state legislators use to pass the laws that govern the state. There is nothing more authentic than watching students sit in desks or stand at podiums that just the day before were being used by the state leadership.

When Does This Activity Occur?

Some organizations conduct Youth and Government as a weeklong program during which students not only make arguments, but also write their bills. Others have students write their bills prior to coming to the Youth and Government event and then spend a couple of days presenting and debating the bills.

Why Should Students Participate?

Youth and Government could be run in a social studies class, especially one that focuses on government. It teaches students the process of getting a bill turned into a law. Students get to hear viewpoints of students from all over the state, and they get to hear students presenting passionately about topics that are meaningful to them, which is how politics works.

Because students have to defend their bills and address any questions that are posed by other legislators, they have to be able to adapt quickly to any situation as well as be able to properly make their argument. Youth and Government involves public speaking in an authentic format beyond the classroom bubble or the safety of an audience students know.

How Do You Run This Activity?

Most Youth and Government groups are developed at the school, although there are some that represent the local YMCA. I ran my Youth and Government group as a before-school extracurricular. Meetings were spent showing students the formatting of the bills they were to write. Then students worked on these independently or with a partner if there were two people sponsoring a bill. After submitting these bills, we worked on the speeches that accompany the bills. We would listen and offer feedback on everything from content, to volume, to persuasiveness, to body language. Other members of the group would ask questions that legislators might ask about the bills at the event in order to prepare students for the unexpected. For more information, visit http://www.ymcayag.org. Most states also have their own website to help to provide advisors with information on how to get students registered.

Business Professionals of America (BPA)

What Is This Activity?

Business Professionals of America (BPA; https://bpa.org) is a cocurricular competition typically run through a career and technical education class. BPA is a competition with nearly 100 events that fall under five categories: finance, business administration, management information systems, digital communication and design, and management, marketing, and communication. According to the BPA (n.d.-b) website, the mission is to:

> enhance student participation in professional, civic, service and social endeavors as they prepare for careers in today's modern business environment. . . . Students involved with BPA participate in various educational programs and activities that offer self-improvement, leadership development, professionalism, community service, career development, public relations, student cooperation, and safety [and] health. (para. 1, 3)

Who Can Be Involved?

BPA is usually implemented through a career and technical education course at the high school level, mostly with juniors and seniors. Students learn the basics of certain aspects of business, which they then use to competently participate in the BPA competitive events. For example, if the focus for the class was multimedia and creation of websites, then those students would compete in that category, trying to make the best business website possible. Students become members of BPA, which costs $14 per person.

Where Does This Activity Take Place?

BPA sponsors several leadership conferences, starting at the regional level, then to the state level, and finally to the national level. The Regional Leadership Conference is held for teams in a nearby location. You can find where there are chapters in your area by visiting https://bpa.org/get-involved/join. At the Regional Leadership Conference, students are evaluated in the various competition areas. Here are some of contests you might find at a regional (BPA, n.d.-a):

- **Video Production Team:** Create a three-to-five (3–5) minute video production, based upon the assigned topic.
- **Graphic Design Promotion:** Develop a theme, illustrate the theme in a logo design, and then utilize the logo in a promotional flyer.
- **Broadcast News Production Team:** Create a three-to-five (3–5) minute news broadcast, containing two (2) different segments (news stories).
- **Presentation Management Team:** Assess use of current desktop technologies and software to prepare and deliver an effective multimedia presentation.
- **Fundamental Word Processing:** Evaluate fundamental skills in word processing and document production.
- **Fundamental Desktop Publishing:** Evaluate knowledge and skills in using desktop publishing software to create a variety of business documents.
- **Business Law & Ethics:** This contest will test the student's knowledge and skills in the areas of ethics, law, business law, and personal law.
- **Extemporaneous Speech:** Demonstrate communication skills in arranging, organizing, and effectively presenting information orally without prior knowledge of the topic.
- **Website Design Team:** The team will work together to create a website based on the assigned topic.

Winners in each of these competitions is determined, and the top teams go to the State Leadership Conference. If students qualify at the state tournament, they are invited to participate in the National Leadership Conference.

When Does This Activity Occur?

The Regional Leadership Conference date is set by the region, but typically occurs in December or January so that teams know who is moving on to the State Leadership Conference.

The State Conference is held a few weeks after all of the regionals have run their tournaments. This is usually in February or March. Many regions, districts, or states opt to also arrange Fall Leadership Conferences in which there is no competition. These conferences are usually less formal and instead offer workshops for areas such as social media etiquette, proper professional dress, public speaking, etc.

The National Leadership Conference is held toward the end of the school year, either late April or beginning of May. Nearly 6,000 students from across the nation compete in more than 71 events.

Why Should Students Participate?

The skills students learn have value beyond the classroom and into students' careers. BPA allows students to prepare for specific career fields in an authentic setting while competing against others. This competition replicates what life will be like in the work force, with employees having to prove their skills and merits.

Because in many cases students have to show a certain level of drive to be able to compete against other students, they have to develop initiative. They have to learn time management because the competition has a deadline to it, they learn to collaborate as a group because many competitions involve a team of students, and they must learn adaptation because they are constantly having to troubleshoot problems and make changes to their products. Even after a team qualifies at states, they have the opportunity to take their product and improve upon it.

The conferences also have a 2-day leadership training during which students may participate in hands-on activities that teach them what makes a good leader and other skills.

How Do You Run This Activity?

Because BPA is usually part of the curriculum for a career and technical education class, the person who runs it is a career/tech teacher. The first part of the year would be talent development. The teacher would want to recognize students with certain talents and then encourage them to compete in that category. For example, if the teacher has a few students who are talented at videography, they would suggest those students take part in the video production team. Or if the teacher has a particularly skilled student in word processing, the fundamental word processing competition would be a good place to demonstrate this.

Ideally, the teacher would find events for all students to participate in and make the necessary arrangements to get students registered and have any fees paid through the school. Then, the teacher would work with those individual teams and students to prepare them for the competition. A lot of the work is done prior to the competition, and the teacher would provide feedback to improve students' performance and to help them to understand the expectations of the competition.

Sometimes this mentorship goes beyond the classroom. When my daughter qualified for the National Leadership Conference, her teacher chaperoned her team as well as some other students to Anaheim, CA, to compete. This involved being gone for a few days. The following year the teacher took them to Dallas. TX. These trips were paid for through the school.

Homegrown Idea—Peer Tutoring Program

What Is This Activity?

A peer tutoring program involves students helping other students with academic areas they are struggling in or are just trying to get better at. This could involve students in the same grade level, with students who are stronger in particular subjects tutoring those who are struggling. This could involve older students offering to tutor younger students. This could also involve teaching general skills that would be beneficial to students, such as how to study, time management, note-taking, organization, or other executive function skills. This could involve something more specific, such as ACT prep or how to write your college application essay. It is important to identify a need that your school has and try to develop the peer tutoring program to meet that need.

It is also important to describe what this AECA is *not*. This is *not* about a student finishing their work early and then helping those students who are struggling with it. This is *not* a good combination, as neither student has offered or asked for this help. Peer tutoring should be voluntary on both sides, and students should receive proper training if they are going to act as peer tutors.

Who Can Be Involved?

Any student can be a tutor. Research has shown that the achievement level of the tutor is not that important. Responsibility is a far more important characteristic to possess. It would require the tutors to be reliable and to make sure they are comfortable enough with a topic to be able to teach it to others. It would teach them responsibility as well as leadership, as many times peer tutors lead by example. This would be a good program for anyone who is interested in pursuing a career in teaching.

As an advisor, you must vet your student candidates to make sure they fit the profile of someone who will be able to deliver what the program is trying accomplish. Your program will need to develop what this profile looks like and what sort of interviews or training will be involved.

Where Does This Activity Take Place?

Depending on how hands-on the program is in regard to the school, this could be offered at the school, either in a classroom or maybe a cafeteria where several groups can spread out and receive tutoring. You could also run it at the local library, where there may be study vestibules and spaces. There is a liability issue, however, when you move the peer tutoring off campus, so it might be a good idea to offer it at the school where an advisor can supervise and keep an eye on things.

When Does This Activity Occur?

This could be before or after school. It could be for a short period of time or encompass the entire school year. It should be consistent, however. For instance, if you are offering peer tutoring for the SAT, your group might offer it every day for 2 weeks leading up to the exam. If instead a student is tutoring someone in French class, this might be a yearlong situation in which the tutor and a student meet once a week, every week. Your tutoring group could also offer the tutoring at a very specific day and time, and then students who would like help can attend the sessions. They might only need a session or two of tutoring to get back on track. Again, this is going to come down to what your peer tutoring group decides is going to be the focus.

In order for students to learn leadership, however, the best case would be that they are assigned a few students whom they work with the entire year and are able to develop a relationship with. This is where the subject matters less and the example the peer tutor sets is more influential.

Why Should Students Participate?

Peer tutoring provides leadership opportunities and skill building for those who are acting as tutors. Skills such as dependability, initiative, time management, and organization are all attributes that good leaders possess. It also feels good to help others. This leaves the peer tutors with a sense of accomplishment. Let's not forget that the students who are receiving the tutoring get help as well. A student might learn something they were unable to in the classroom and begin to develop a sense of confidence. It is sometimes easier to ask a peer a question instead of the teacher, and peer tutoring gives students that opportunity.

How Do You Run This Activity?

An effective peer tutoring program should have clear goals as to what your student tutors are trying to accomplish, as well as a structure or organized plan to make sure services are consistent and accessible. I think the important thing is that you not just place high-ability students with lower achieving students and hoping for the best. Even if a tutor has a good understanding of a topic does not mean they are able to communicate their understanding to someone else. Your program would best be served by providing training for the tutors before they begin working with students.

This training should also be offered throughout the tutoring program. The advisor would be most effective having meetings with their peer tutors at least once a month to check on how things are going and to offer any support that might be needed. The tutoring might include how to:

1. develop a plan for learning,
2. provide positive verbal feedback that also is corrective,
3. motivate a student,
4. use problem-solving techniques to develop a strategy that will help the student,
5. be empathetic and understanding, and
6. build mutual respect and trust.

The advisor for this program would then need to do as is expected of the peer tutors, which is to lead by example. This would include modeling what good teaching looks like when you are training them, providing corrective feedback in your meetings, and role-playing tough situations so that they can develop problem-solving skills for similar situations.

Something Extra to Think About

There isn't a test students can take or book they can read to become accomplished leaders; they have to be given opportunities to actually lead. It is important to identify those who show the skills of leadership and encourage them. Many students gifted in leadership will naturally gravitate to AECAs like the ones mentioned in this chapter. Even if all of your students are not going to be leaders, the aforementioned skills will benefit them in other ways.

Here are five things you can do to help your students develop leadership skills:

1. Put them in authentic, high-pressure situations.

2. Involve them in collaborative activities.
3. Give them chances to show initiative.
4. Have them engage in activities that require adaptability.
5. Develop grit in students.

CHAPTER 7

Creative Thinking

In many states, in addition to gifted testing in the core subject areas of ELA, math, science, and social studies, districts also try to identify students who are creative thinkers. A lot of times educators hear this term and think that this means *artistically* creative students, or those who are good at art. That is only part of what creative thinking is. Creative thinking is a different way of looking at something, coming up with unique solutions to a problem. A creative thinker is the student who comes up with a solution no one else has considered. And as off-the-wall a response as it may seem, the student has a sound rationalization for why they chose that solution.

The challenge that many school districts face is how to serve these creative thinkers. Is there a class or a curriculum that can be used to ensure these children are being challenged to use their gift of creative thinking? Unfortunately, many of the core content areas do not have much room for creative thinking. ELA classes are putting more emphasis on informational text. Many math programs show step-by-step ways to solve problems, rather than giving students the space to try to figure out concepts for themselves. Social studies may dive into the past without letting students come up with creative solutions for the future. In science, students work on a lab, following the directions provided for them rather than being given free rein to run the experiment any way they choose.

How do we provide students with ways to build and develop their creative thinking? By offering AECAs that are more open ended that require students to use and extend their creative thinking abilities.

Chess Club

What Is This Activity?

Offering a chess club can be as simple as providing a place where students are exposed to the game. It can be set up differently depending on student skill level. I have run some clubs where a majority of students did not know how to play, so I spent most of the club time teaching them the basic moves, with the end goal being that they could play a game against an opponent without any intervention. I have run some clubs where the members were more advanced and understood how to play. With this group I would set up games between students, allowing them the opportunity to build their skills with the game. We would occasionally look at some basic strategies or techniques to improve their chess thinking, but this level of club was very recreational. For my most advanced students, we would compete locally against other schools or chess teams, sometimes even going to national tournaments. You could also form a club that involves students of all ability levels, allowing you to differentiate activities and competitions to match their abilities, much like you would in the regular classroom for groups of students of various skill levels.

Who Can Be Involved?

The great thing about chess is that you can teach the basic premise to almost anyone, even to very young kids, and they can catch on quite quickly. After students learn the basic rules and moves, you can scaffold in higher level chess thinking skills. You can teach students to slow the game down and to think about the moves they are making and to anticipate the moves their opponent might make. This level of strategizing requires students to think creatively.

You can start chess with kindergarteners, which I have done. You can also have high school students playing chess so that the club runs the entire gamut of school-age children. You can involve any number of participants. You just need to have the appropriate number of boards and sets of pieces. You can have advanced players and beginners. This is why I love to run a chess club. It fits so many different groups.

Where Does This Activity Take Place?

You can use nearly any type of room to run a chess club, provided you have the supplies on hand (i.e., the appropriate number of chess sets). For some of the schools I work with, I spoke to the PTO to fund the purchase of the boards and pieces. Other times is was funded through the gifted department. These sets became the property of the school so that students can play during indoor recess. We made members of the club the stewards of these chess boards, making sure no one was damaging the sets and that all pieces were put back.

Another "where" you might have to consider is that, if you decide to host a district tournament, is there a central or convenient building it can take place? Finding a space should not be difficult, as you can use the cafeteria or set up tables in the gymnasium. My students and I hosted a couple of these tournaments, which involved me using the gymnasium and setting up enough tables to accommodate play. We also used the cafeteria as a place where students and family members could hang out between rounds. Unlike many AECA events, most chess tournaments do not allow spectators to watch the actual chess matches. You can also provide skittles rooms for chess clubs who bring multiple students. This meant delegating a classroom for that chess club. Overall it was a fairly simple event to organize, and we actually made money for the school to fund future chess clubs.

For really competitive teams, you might find yourself going to tournaments around the state or even out of state. You can find a listing of national tournaments at https://new.uschess.org/national-events-calendar. Tournaments are not necessary for a chess club, but they do provide students with valuable experience and a chance to play people they normally wouldn't play. The tournament atmosphere also provides authenticity. Most tournaments do a pretty good job of grouping students based on skill. My daughter played Scholastic chess tournaments for a few years, and I was always impressed with how they were run, how they differentiated the chess ability so that kids weren't getting trounced by someone really good if they were a beginner, and how many kids were involved.

When Does This Activity Occur?

Chess club can be held every week, every other week, or even once a month. The more chess students play, the better they are going to get. So if you want your chess team to improve, having more frequent chess meetings would be preferable. If you take too long between chess meetings, especially with the younger beginner students, they may forget how to make the moves and you may have to start over with instruction. With groups that can only meet once a month I always show them how to download free chess apps on their smartphones or tablets so that they can play without needing a person or a meeting to do so.

It is always nice to provide a year-end tournament for those participating in the club to participate in. This can be something as simple as having them play against one another to determine the champion.

Most tournament formats involve five rounds. Winners from each round are awarded a point, with boards that tie receiving only half a point. Then, in the second round, you match up the students with the same number of points to play one another, and you do this each round until the player who has the most points after five rounds is named the champion. In official United States Chess Federation-sanctioned tournaments, there are all sorts of tie breakers and ways to differentiate competitors who have the same amount of points, but I recommend keeping the tie-breaking options simple at the school level.

If you have chess clubs at multiple schools in the district such as I had, you could organize a district tournament where teams play against one another. You could organize a tournament against a nearby school district. You could even check your area to see if there are sanctioned chess tournaments available. For a nominal fee, individuals and teams can compete in these for individual or team trophies. These tournaments run throughout the year so they can be an ongoing opportunity, depending on how competitive your team is. You can search online or visit the United States Chess Federation site (http://www.uschess.org/tlas/upcoming.php) to find tournaments near you.

Why Should Students Participate?

Chess is great for creative thinking because there is no one correct way to play chess. The possibilities are endless. In fact, after making the first move on the chess board, there are 400 possible board setups. After that turn, there are 197,742 possibilities, and after that, 121 million. In the time it takes students to make four moves, they have opened up so many possibilities, some that will lead to their victory and some that will not.

More than that, students have to anticipate the moves their opponent is going to make and either stop or trap them as their opponent tries to do the same. This requires creative thinking at its finest. Chess also:

- teaches students how to win and lose,
- improves spatial skills,
- can help students learn focus,
- develops memory,
- increases students' long-term thinking skills,
- builds confidence, and
- develops problem-solving skills.

Gifted students benefit from playing chess because it also teaches grit. Grit is the ability to run into an obstacle, or even failure, and bounce back and persevere. Chess is all about learning from failures. This is why people who seriously study chess look at past games to see what worked and what didn't. During the first few tournaments my daughter played in, she rarely won and we were happy when she got a bye (i.e., a round she did not play but received a half-point or full point for if, for example, the tournament had an odd number of players). Eventually, however, she learned enough from her less effective performances to begin to win against opponents, eventually placing 16th in her age and rating division at a national tournament. Now, as an adult, she is able to persevere when something doesn't go her way, and I believe a large part of this is due to her years of playing chess. The game taught her grit.

How Do You Run This Activity?

Running a chess club depends on your skill level and that of your students. I know enough about chess to be able to teach the basics, including some strategies, to beginner and intermediate players. However, there have been some players, some only in fifth grade, whose skill surpassed my own, and I felt I did not have much to offer them. In cases such as this, I brought in a chess instructor who knew a lot more strategies to teach. There also are many online chess tutorials that students can watch to learn how to become better players, including many videos on YouTube. There also are a lot of great chess lessons to be found at https://www.chess.com/lessons.

Future Problem Solving Program International

What Is This Activity?

Future Problem Solving Program International (FPSPI; https://www.fpspi.org) is an international program in which students solve a problem using a six-step model, which teaches critical and creative thinking, problem solving, and decision making. The problems deal with technological, geopolitical, and social trends, and ask students to imagine what trends might emerge in 20–30 years. The idea is that students will develop solutions to problems they might actually face when they are older.

The six-step model includes:

1. Identify challenges that exist in a given situation.
2. Pick a high-impact "Underlying Problem" to focus on, formulated as an attainable goal that addresses the problem.
3. Brainstorm solutions to the Underlying Problem.
4. Develop criteria that measure solutions' positive impact on people affected by the Underlying Problem.
5. Evaluate and rank the solutions using the criteria.
6. Develop an elaborated Action Plan based on the highest-ranking solution. ("Future Problem Solving Program International," 2020, sec. 1, para. 1)

Some past FPSPI problems have included sleep patterns, gamification, poverty, drones, coping with stress, spread of infectious diseases, educational disparities, identity theft, and more.

Who Can Be Involved?

FPSPI is for students grades 4–12. FPSPI also offers curriculum, including *Action-Based Problem Solving* for grades K–3. "Action-based Problem Solving" (AbPS) teaches a simpler version of the problem-solving process, including how to write ideas. Once students master this they can move on to the problem-solving experience curriculum, which targets grades 5–8 and helps them to promote critical thinking in the 21st century.

There are four different contests students can compete in for FPSPI. First is the Global Issues Problem Solving (FPSPI, n.d.-b), which is for individuals or a team of up to four students. It has contests in the junior, middle, and senior age divisions. For this, students get a Future Scene, which is an imagined scenario of that year's topic set 20–40 years in the future. Students are then supposed to develop creative possibilities for solving the problem.

The second contest is the Community Problem Solving (FPSPI, n.d.-b). This can be for an individual or a team of any size, and is for the junior, middle, and senior divisions. The idea here is that students identify a problem in their own community that they analyze over the course of the school year and try to determine the way to best solve it.

Then there is the Scenario Performance and Scenario Writing (FPSPI, n.d.-b). The Scenario Performance involves individuals, either at the junior, middle, or senior levels, developing and performing an oral story of up to 5 minutes, with the main idea of the story being students' future projection about one of the annual topics. Scenario Writing is similar, but instead of performing the story, students write it, using no more than 1,500 words.

Where Does This Activity Take Place?

There are affiliates all across the U.S., each of which is responsible for conducting the competition for those in their geographic area. To find your state's affiliate you can go to https://www.fpspi.org/slider/find-an-affiliate. Depending on how large the area or the demand, there may be a regional, state, and international levels of competition. Most have state competitions first. These are held in various locations, so again, finding your state's FPSPI website will be a good way to learn where this is held. Students and teams that perform the best there are invited to the international conference. The international conference chooses a new location every 2 years.

When Does This Activity Occur?

The number of levels of competition for your state will determine the timeline for getting a team ready. The state competition usually occurs between late March to mid-April so that students have time to prepare and raise funds to attend the international conference held in May or June. If the state is large enough to have regionals as well, these would need to be held beforehand, typically in February.

Why Should Students Participate?

FPSPI was founded by Dr. E. Paul Torrance. Torrance is well-known in the gifted education community for his work on creativity and developing it amongst students. He designed FPSPI for that very purpose, to develop creative thinking by having students work toward a solution to an ill-structured problem. Because of this, some schools use the FPSPI curriculum in classrooms to service students with high creative thinking abilities because the curriculum uses the same model as the Torrance Tests of Creative Thinking for identifying gifted students.

FPSPI also covers all of the 21st-century skills known as the 4 C's:

- **Creativity and Innovation:** Problem-solving situations are set in the future to encourage inventive thinking. Students learn to look at situations from a variety of perspectives. Creativity is essential as they generate challenges and develop multiple ideas for solutions to pressing problems.
- **Critical Thinking and Problem Solving:** Students use analysis to gain an understanding of issues in today's world and to comprehend the significant aspects of complex situations set in the future. Problem-solving skills are applied as they focus on possible solutions and develop Action Plans for those situations.
- **Communication and Collaboration:** Students collaborate in teams while learning about the issues and while applying their problem-solving skills. Clear and articulate communication is developed while working with a team, an essential skill for our future leaders. (FPSPI, n.d.-a, sec. 3)

How Do You Run This Activity?

A coach can be as involved as they want to be. If a team has been together for a few years, the students are most likely familiar enough with the program to run things themselves with some sideline guidance from the advisor. If a team is new to FPSPI, the advisor may need to be more involved in order to explain the process. Advisors will have to have a firm understanding of how the competition works. They can learn this by attending FPSPI events in their area, or affiliates many times provide training for those new to FPSPI. As an advisor, you would just need to contact your state's affiliate and inquire if and when these trainings are offered. Some courses your state's affiliate might offer include:

- New Coach Training,
- CmPS Coach Training,
- CmPS Training,

- Advanced Coached Training, and
- Scenario Coach Training.

In addition, there are materials that can be purchased on the FPSPI website, including a coach's manual, examples of past winners' solutions, and curriculum that can be used.

Destination Imagination

What Is This Activity?

Destination Imagination (DI; https://www.destinationimagination.org) is a global program that tasks students with solving challenges. Teams register with the national affiliate of DI and receive a passport number and materials for the challenge in which they are enrolled. The students must then create a skit that demonstrates the elements of the challenge as well as specific skills. Through this, they utilize higher level creative thinking abilities to develop a solution.

DI (n.d.) offers various challenges to choose from, each with a different focus, including the:
- Technical Challenge,
- Scientific Challenge,
- Engineering Challenge,
- Fine Arts Challenge,
- Improvisational Challenge, and
- Service Learning Challenge.

Who Can Be Involved?

DI is for students of all ages. When competing, there are four different age ranges:
- Rising Stars: Pre-K–grade 2
- Elementary Level: grades K–5
- Middle Level: grades 6–8
- Secondary Level: grades 9–12

You can have teams with students from different grades, but you must register based on your oldest team member. In other words, if you have a team of six fifth graders and one sixth grader, that team must compete in the middle level.

Teams are made up of 4–7 individuals. The members of the team are the only ones allowed to develop ideas for solving their challenge. The team also includes a team manager, who is there to organize practices, make sure students follow the correct structure of the challenge, and provide feedback when asked, but not to provide ideas. A team can be penalized for interference if someone outside of the group contributes to their solution.

Where Does This Activity Take Place?

After preparing for several months, teams register with a local affiliate. Most states are divided geographically into regions, with each region hosting its own tournament. Teams attend these tournaments, and those that score the best on their challenge are invited to go to the state competition. The state competition is hosted usually in a single location. You can find your state website at https://www.destinationimagination.org/challenge-program/locations. This will help you determine where the state tournament is being hosted as well as what region you belong to. From the state competition, the best teams go to the global competition, which has been held in Kansas City, MO, in the past few years.

When Does This Activity Occur?

Like most competitions, the dates of events have to work backward from the final competition, which is at the global level. Globals is an appropriate name, as 15-plus countries take part in the event that is held toward the end of the school year in late May. In order for teams to qualify for the Globals, state tournaments need to be conducted in March or April so that those going can raise the necessary money. The tournament can be a bit pricey, costing $5,500 per team.

The state tournament is populated by the teams that won their regional tournament, which is held either in February or March. There are some states that do not have regionals and simply hold a state tournament for everyone who wishes to participate, such as Kansas, Wyoming, and West Virginia. Other states have many regions, such as Texas with 16 and Ohio with 11.

Why Should Students Participate?

First and foremost, Destination Imagination is fun. As students construct sets, develop solutions, memorize lines, and put on their production, they also learn valuable 21st-century skills. Destination Imagination readily combines two of these skills—creativity and problem solving. After all, it is a creative problem-solving competition. Through the competition, students also develop valuable critical thinking skills.

In addition to the central challenge in which students have to solve a problem that they work on for most of the school year, DI has another component: the instant challenge. Teams do not know what the instant challenge will be when they arrive at the tournament. Typically, students are led to a room, are told the instant challenge, and then must immediately try to solve it with minimal preparation time. This teaches students adaptation, a skill that will be often encountered in the real world. As much planning as we might do in our lives, things come up, things change, or things fall apart. Students must know how to adapt to changes, but they will have difficulty doing so if they have not developed the mechanisms. How many times in the classroom are students asked to adapt at a moment's notice? Not as much as they should. By participating in this AECA, students are exposed to this valuable skill. The instant challenge is right up the alley of gifted students, which is why I like this facet of the competition. It requires improvisational skills and thinking on the spot, something most gifted students excel at, although they do not often get the chance to use these skills.

How Do You Run This Activity?

I have run more than 30 teams for DI, and probably the toughest thing is to allow the students to create the solution solely on their own with no input from you. That means if a team is not getting their skit written or hasn't made a prop they need, it is not up to you to do it for them. Students come up with the solution on their own, they might fail on their own, and the product needs to be theirs.

There are a few things I have learned over the years:
1. **Read the challenge carefully.** There are so many requirements that, if you don't know your challenge really well, you might overlook a few things. This can end up haunting you if judges are required to score on any aspect you or your team missed.
2. **Provide space for the team.** The main job of the team manager during practices is to provide space for students to bounce ideas off of one another or to provide resources students may need to build sets or props. Oh, and it doesn't hurt to also provide some snacks every now and then.
3. **Check for clarifications.** Clarifications are questions other teams have asked about the challenge that DI then makes decisions about, clarifying and sometimes altering what teams can and cannot do. As the team manager, you are expected to look these up. One year I did not, and the

team did something that a clarification said was not allowed, which I did not know, and we were penalized for it.

4. **Look over the Rules of the Road.** The Rules of the Road is the handbook of how all challenges will be conducted and scored (see https://resources.destinationimagination.org/resources.php). Being familiar with the rules will allow your team to avoid mistakes and be better prepared.

Rube Goldberg Machine Contest

What Is This Activity?

A Rube Goldberg Machine is a machine that performs a fairly simple task in a rather complex manner. Rube Goldberg machines are named after a cartoonist who would depict devices performing simple tasks in indirect convoluted ways (see https://www.rubegoldberg.com/image-gallery-licensing for some examples). To help you see how a Rube Goldberg machine works, you can watch the following video, which features the machine with the Guinness World Record for the longest such device: https://www.youtube.com/watch?v=RBOqfLVCDv8.

The Rube Goldberg Machine Contest (https://www.rubegoldberg.com/contests-landing) tasks teams with creating their own machine that accomplishes the act that the year's theme is based on. Some of these from past years include (Rube Goldberg, n.d.-b):

- 2020: Turn off a light.
- 2019: Put money in a piggy bank.
- 2018: Pour a bowl of cereal.
- 2017: Apply an adhesive bandage.
- 2016: Open an umbrella.
- 2015: Erase a chalkboard.
- 2014: Zip a zipper.
- 2013: Hammer a nail.

Generally, teams must build a device that can perform the task in a minimum of 20 steps and run its course within 2 minutes. Teams are scored on whether the machine works in two out of three attempts, as well as on the general impression of the team's theme and how well the team works together.

Who Can Be Involved?

The Rube Goldberg Machine Contest has several divisions of competition separated by age bracket: ages 8–11, ages 11–14, and ages 14–18. There is also an all-ages family division (Rube Goldberg, n.d.-a). All teams need to have an advisor and have at least three members, but no more than 14.

Where Does This Activity Take Place?

There are two types of contests—live and online. In live contests, teams build their machine, transport it to a host site, and compete against other teams. Any school is eligible to host a tournament as long as it provides judges, awards, and the proper space to host the competition. The teams that finish in the top three in their division are reported to Rube Goldberg, Inc. As the advisor, you can find a host site near you by visiting https://www.rubegoldberg.com/contests/find-a-host. Those who win the tournament are then eligible to compete in the live finals. The finals move location from year to year. Past locations include Lawrenceburg, IN, Chicago, IL, and Columbus, OH.

For teams who may not be able to travel to a host site, there is also the option of an online contest in which students build their machine and film it. Teams register for the contest, pay the registration fee, and build a team page. Teams must submit two 3-minute videos of machine runs without any edits. Once their video is submitted, they are evaluated on its performance by judges and people's choice voting (Rube Goldberg, n.d.-a). (*Note.* For 2021, the Rube Goldberg Machine Contest moved entirely online due to the COVID-19 pandemic. Be sure to visit the contest's webpage for details on the year in which you intend to compete: https://www.rubegoldberg.com.)

When Does This Activity Occur?

The live tournaments can take place anywhere from the beginning of October to mid-March. They have to be finished by mid-March because the finals are hosted in the month of April. Visit the following webpage for contest calendars: https://www.rubegoldberg.com/contests/schedule-deadlines.

The online contest can be performed at any time within the school year, and the team just needs to be sure to submit its videos. The videos are usually due in the spring. The contest then eliminates teams over the course of three rounds. At the end of the third round, a champion is crowned. There is also a people's choice voting, where people can view the machines and vote for the ones they like the best. The winners decided by both the judges and the public are usually announced in April or May.

Why Should Students Participate?

Creating a Rube Goldberg machine requires a lot of creative thinking. There are millions of outcomes to choose from as well as numerous different materials to use. These endless possibilities are a gold mine for gifted students who are capable of imagining different solutions. Students also have to determine how all of the parts of their machine are going to go together. If students are going to impress the judges, they need to creatively design and construct their machine. Excelling at this competition takes artistry, storytelling, and a sense of humor because the reality is that these machines are ridiculous and needlessly complex.

Students also learn communication, problem solving, and collaboration, all valuable 21st-century skills. There is also the element of the engineering design process (see p. 62), especially the improve phase. Students get three attempts at getting their machine to work properly. After any failure, students need to determine what changes they need to make in order to achieve success.

How Do You Run This Activity?

You would best serve your students by providing them with a structure, giving them resources, and then getting out of their way. The Rube Goldberg Machine Contest explicitly states that everything, from the ideas, to the construction, to even moving it to the competition site, should be done by the students (Rube Goldberg, n.d.-a).

You could start the club by looking at what a Rube Goldberg machine looks like. There are plenty of examples on YouTube as well as in the contest's collection of videos located at https://www.rubegoldberg.com/video. Then, let students brainstorm all sorts of ideas and experiment with all sorts of possibilities. You might want to have some general materials for them to use, such as:

- aluminum foil,
- plastic containers,
- cardboard,
- water bottles,
- toilet paper or paper towel tubes,
- cereal or cake mix boxes,
- beverage cans or soup cans,
- dominoes,

- funnels,
- marbles,
- golf balls,
- toy cars,
- string,
- buckets, and
- cups or bowls.

Once students settle on a design, I would think a good amount of your effort would be procuring materials for students to use. You could either ask students to bring these materials in themselves, you can ask for donations, or ask if your school has a budget to purchase them.

There is a cost for the local contest of $395 per team. It is another $400 to go to the finals. Teams are encouraged to seek out sponsors or fundraising events to cover these costs, as well as any additional materials costs.

Homegrown Idea— Dungeons and Dragons

What Is This Activity?

Dungeons and Dragons, or D&D for short, is a fantasy role-playing game in which participants assume the part of a character and are led through an adventure with the guidance of a Dungeon Master. Participants take part in adventures and must roll the dice to determine their consequences. D&D provides the structure for the adventure, but the Dungeon Master and participants create a lot of the storytelling. There isn't really a winner or loser in the traditional sense of those terms. The group creates the adventure together, requiring collaboration and creative thinking.

There are lots of rules for Dungeons and Dragons and lots of different sets you can purchase. For an overview of the basics, you can go to https://www.dndbeyond.com/sources/basic-rules. The basic structure of D&D, however, is fairly simple:

1. The Dungeon Master describes the environment, whether it is a spooky castle, an exploding volcano, or a dangerous tavern, as well as options that are available. Sometimes the location can be represented by a map with figurines representing the players.

2. Players describe what they want to do and what actions they wish to take. Sometimes they are group actions, sometimes individual actions. Players then roll the dice to see how successful their action was.
3. After an action is taken, the Dungeon Master narrates the consequences of the action, and then the cycle starts all over again.

Who Can Be Involved?

Anyone can be involved, but given the sword and sorcery aspect, as well as the battles and fighting, Dungeons and Dragons is best suited for middle school students and up. You don't have to be a fan of sword and sorcery in order to enjoy Dungeons and Dragons, but it typically appeals to people who enjoy fantasy.

Where Does This Activity Take Place?

Dungeons and Dragons can be conducted almost anywhere that has a table set up for the group so that rolling dice and laying out a map/board, if applicable, are possible. A regular classroom would be great depending on the size of your club. You can put desks together or use the floor as larger workspaces if you have several students taking part in the same adventure.

When Does This Activity Occur?

Dungeons and Dragons does not have a year-end tournament like other AECAs. If you hold weekly meetings, whoever shows up that week is going to participate in an adventure. You can rotate who holds the role of Dungeon Master from week to week, or if you find some students who seem to have a knack for the role, they can serve as designated Dungeon Masters.

Students can take part in a new adventure each time the group meets, or if they prefer longer adventures, they can continue the next week from where they left off previously. It is really up to the students to take the adventure wherever they want.

Why Should Students Participate?

Dungeons and Dragons fully involves creative thinking and, at the same time, requires that students be good storytellers. Students' stories must have a beginning, middle, and end, their story must be told in a logical order, and the more details provided the better the story is.

In addition, Dungeons and Dragons teaches:

1. **Problem solving:** The exciting thing about D&D is that you never know what is going to happen next, and quite often it is not something you were expecting. Learning how to solve problems quickly and putting the solutions into action also improves students' initiative.
2. **Teamwork:** Participants are not working against one another but instead are encouraged to work together. This teaches students that they can be more successful collaborating with a group on certain tasks, rather than trying to solve everything on their own.
3. **Creativity:** Although the Dungeon Master is running most of the story, there is a large degree of creativity when participants are deciding what to do next. Thinking of something that lacks creativity could get a player in trouble. D&D encourages creative responses and solutions in order to be successful.
4. **Improvisation:** Having to react to whatever is thrown their way or figuring out how to pivot when something doesn't go their way leads students toward building the skill of adaptation.
5. **Empathy:** D&D requires students to live in someone else's shoes. It allows students to understand the perspective of someone else, as well as the perspectives of the students they are playing with.

How Do You Run This Activity?

A lot of the time is spent creating the characters students will be using for their adventures. You can find kits in which the characters are already created, but that can take away from some of the joy of students getting to use their creativity to develop these characters.

The only real supplies you are going to need are enough sets of dice for multiple groups to have adventures, as well as a player's handbook so that the rules are handy. There are six different dice used in D&D, including one that is 4-sided, 6-sided, 8-sided, 10-sided, 12-sided, and 20-sided. There are a lot of premade adventures out there for purchase, which often contain the story, non-playing characters, and the monsters participants might encounter throughout the adventure. If you want to have your club be about creative thinking, allowing students to create their own would be best.

Something Extra to Think About

Creative thinking is not something we put a lot of priority on in our schools, and yet is a skill that will greatly benefit our students if learned well. Businesses are looking for creative thinkers because there are several things they can bring to an organization:

- **Creative thinking helps one stay ahead:** There is a saying that if you are on the cutting edge, it is difficult to sit down. Businesses have to be coming up with the new product or take the products they already have and market them in fresh ways. It is not about just keeping up; it is about getting ahead of the competition.
- **Creative thinking promotes problem solving:** I have discussed the importance of problem solving numerous times in this book, and another thing to consider is not just solving the problem, but also implementing the solution. This is also a crucial skill to develop in students.
- **Creative thinking increases productivity:** 3M encourages 15% time, during which employees are encouraged to work on projects that are interesting to them and where they can be most creative. During this time, some of 3M's most popular products have been developed, such as Post-It Notes, clear bandages, and painter's tape that prevents the paint from bleeding (Goetz, 2011). None of that would have happened had 3M not been willing to support these creative ideas and provide the time for their development.
- **Creative thinking makes people feel appreciated:** When workers are allowed to be creative, they feel as though their voice is heard and feel appreciated.

Now imagine you could provide these same advantages to your students and their learning process. How powerful would that be for them? How valuable would they be to a future employer?

CHAPTER 8

Final Thoughts

As much as I would like the scenario presented in the beginning of this book in which academic extracurricular activities get the same or more attention than sports do in our schools, I realize this is unrealistic. After all, there is not a multitude of television channels devoted to AECAs like there are for sports. That is why it is up to educators like you to provide these opportunities for students and be the champion of these activities. For most sports programs, when a coach leaves the position, there is someone else ready to take their place. The same cannot be said for those who coach or advise AECAs. Oftentimes, there is not someone to pick up the mantle, and as a result, the program simply gets discontinued at the expense of the students.

More than that, students expect for there to be sports offered at their school. You hear it on the announcements, and you see the trophies in the front lobby and when the school tweets every time someone signs their national letter of intent. Students are aware of what sports are available and how their skillset fits into it. After all, if you ask someone if your school has a basketball team, 10 out of

10 students are going to know the answer is yes. AECAs, on the other hand, are not as in the spotlight. Sure, you might see some signs around school letting students know there is a mock trial team or a message rolling along the bottom of the school's announcements letting students know there is a physics club. If you asked those same 10 students whether the school has a Destination Imagination team, most probably would not know unless they were members of the team themselves. Schools, students, and the media don't do a very good job of making people aware of these academic extracurriculars. There are no signs when coming into town announcing that the Odyssey of the Mind team finished first in the state, but the sports championship signs may stay up for years.

I am not making sports the bad guy in this situation. No, sports are not to blame for being well recognized and getting more of the attention in the extracurricular activity realm. The blame for this comes down to the adults. Are teachers and administration doing their best to make the student body aware of what activities are available to them? Are the central office staff attending these academic events even though they always seem to be able to make the football games or other sporting events? Is the school willing to provide compensation for those people willing to give up their valuable time so that they can advise AECAs? Is the media prepared to report on the students competing in academic extracurriculars and their amazing accomplishments? Are parents willing to encourage their children to participate in these academic extracurriculars and committing to picking their children up from school in the evening or transporting them to activities on the weekend?

We, the adults, need to do a better job in giving AECAs their just due. It starts with people such as yourself, willing to pick up this book and take on the mantle of an AECA. You do so knowing you will not get the recognition other extracurriculars will. Even if there is compensation, it will not be worth the time you are providing to students and the sacrifices you will make to ensure that they are ready. What you will know is that you are doing what is best for kids. You are providing an opportunity for a child who normally may not be in extracurriculars. You are providing an outlet for a passion that otherwise would have been smothered in the day-to-day activities of typical academia. You are providing them the chance to make life-long friends in their teammates.

Because you are willing or considering taking on such an endeavor, let me give you these final thoughts that might help you in your journey.

Rely on the Kindness of Strangers

When you are first starting out in any AECA, it can be difficult to help your students when you don't have a good grasp of the activity yourself because you may be learning along with them. You can, of course, watch all of the videos provided by an organization or attend the local tournaments to get a better understanding of how activity or competition works, but there is no substitute for talking with someone who has experience. I came across many people while researching this book who were more than willing to give me some of their time to explain to me how the AECA they were advising works. These were teachers in my own district, advisors from nationally recognized programs, and state and national coordinators. It was amazing how much time these obviously busy people were able to provide me with so that I could understand their AECA. Every email I sent, every phone call I made, and every request for an interview was answered.

There will be people like that in your own state—either advisors from other schools who have been running an academic extracurricular for years, members of your regional or state board who are more than welcome to lend a helping hand, or people who run the national site or competition if the organization you are interested in reaches that level. You should not be afraid or embarrassed to reach out and ask for help. You can make the process easier by determining what questions you need answered. What are you unsure about, or what aspects of preparing for the competition or activity don't make sense to you? Don't be afraid or unwilling to go to a practice, or if you know you are going to run an AECA next school year, check out the regional or state competition the year before you take over or implement the program. Seeing an AECA in action makes it easier to understand, and having someone you can ask questions of is ever so helpful.

Value of Finding Advocates/Allies

There are 30 AECAs shared in this book. There is no way you can do them all, so it would be important to find one or a couple that resonate with you and channel your own passions. If, however, you would like to provide more opportunities for students to participate in a variety of AECAs, find teachers or community members who would be willing to advise a team. That means if you would like to start a mock trial team, reach out to local law firms to see if anyone would be willing to take that on. If you want to have students participate in WordMasters, have a meeting with the English department and see if any teachers would be willing to have their classes participate. If you have a parent who is heavily involved in an AECA because of their child and you know the advisor is stepping away the following season, ask if the parent would be willing to take over because they already know the program so well. Find potential advisors, whether they be teachers or community members who were previously involved in the AECA, and recruit them. I found a teacher in my district who had done

Odyssey of the Mind, and when we were looking for volunteers for Destination Imagination, which is very similar, she was excited to get involved.

Many teachers may be interested in running an AECA but are unsure of how to start. Teachers who are new to the profession can also be great advocates. They may be eager to help students find their place in an AECA because they, themselves, want to find their place in the district by getting to know students and the school better. You might find a teacher who becomes truly invested in the AECA and becomes a long-term advisor for your students.

There is a lot of power in the act of asking, especially through a personal appeal. In other words, if you are looking for someone to run the MATHCOUNTS team, rather than putting out a general email to the math department to see if anyone would be interested, approach teachers individually and ask them if they would be willing. It is a lot easier to ignore an email than it is a direct request.

For someone considering being an advisor, there is always the fear of not knowing what one is doing that prevents them from taking it on. This obstacle just requires a little encouragement from the correct person and support either through resources or time to turn this person into an advocate for the AECA.

Recruit, Recruit, Recruit

When trying to get students involved in AECAs, it is best not to just offer the club and hope students will join. You might have to do a little purposeful recruiting. Just as a coach for sports would seek out the best athletes for their respective sports, you should do the same for your AECA. For example, let's say you want to offer preparing for Scholastic Art & Writing Awards as an AECA. Rather than just posting a flyer, go to the ELA teachers and ask who their strong writers are. Then go to these students and encourage them to be involved. Or if you are trying to assemble a team for FIRST LEGO Robotics, see if there are any students who have shown a propensity for STEM work and inquire with them if they would be interested in taking it to the next level.

Hold informational meetings to inform students about the AECA. This could be done during homerooms or study halls or other small time blocks. You only need 5 to 10 minutes to explain what it is. If you are trying to recruit members for Model United Nations, ask the social studies teachers if you could come into their classroom for a few minutes to explain what it is or show a short video that explains how it works. Sometimes this might be an evening event. When I was trying to recruit students and parents to participate in Destination Imagination, I invited everyone in the district to come to an hourlong informational meeting, where I went over the basics, had a team from the year before perform a central challenge, and fielded questions.

Have an AECA fair at the beginning of the school year where different clubs set up tables and students visit booths to hear what each club has to offer. You can show videos, display products, and have conversations with students about what is involved in each club.

Get existing members to recruit their friends. Having students recruit other students is always a good idea because the teacher tends to talk about academic aspects, while students will express the fun stuff they get to do, making the AECA more enticing. Or they may be aware of a student who will have a strong aptitude for the AECA that has escaped your attention and bring them in.

Involving Parents/Community

Even though you might be the coordinator of the AECA, you might need some help in its execution. For instance, if you have put together a Science Olympiad team or a speech and debate team, it will be nearly impossible to give attention to all of the various categories students can compete in. Bringing in parents who have know-how or someone who is an expert to help will be hugely beneficial to you. So you might bring in an engineer to work with students who have taken on those challenges in Science Olympiad, or ask an actor to work with your dramatic interpretation speech participants. Having DECA students work with a small business owner or having Future City Builders talk to a city planner will provide them with valuable real-world insight.

You might need to recruit parents and community members to act as judges. Destination Imagination requires every team to provide an appraiser for the tournament. Without this, the team would face a deduction, so finding people to fill these spots is important. Or if you are going to host a Rube Goldberg Machine Contest, having parents who make sure that events run smoothly and that people know where they are going, and who even direct traffic would be helpful. Or if the Invention Convention needs judges, you can find fellow teachers, parents, or community members to volunteer. If your culture club is hosting a community night, getting parents from different cultural backgrounds to be willing to bring in food dishes is always a hit.

Involving parents could be as simple as having a snack list for your meetings with a different parent responsible for bringing something in for each week's practice, or using parents for transportation if the school is not willing to provide it.

Spreading the Word/Honoring the Accomplishments

In order for others to hear about the wonderful accomplishments of your AECAs, you will have to be their loudest advocate. This means making sure news gets on the announcements about the success of different clubs. This means contacting the local press and seeing if they would be willing to do a story on a team's performance. This means lobbying the school board and making sure they are honoring AECA teams that do well in their competition. This means tweeting or using other forms of social media to make members of the community aware of students' accomplishments. Without your efforts to share news, no one may know. My daughter competed in Business Professionals of America website design and finished third in the nation—not third in the state (though her team was first in the state), but third *in the nation.* But other than a couple of tweets, there was little to no mention made of this remarkable accomplishment. Our football team, which won their state title, was provided with a ceremony honoring its great feat that the entire community turned out for, a write-up in the paper, and a sign greeting anyone who comes into our good town. What made all of that possible? People doing their part to get the word out.

Spreading the word about your students' accomplishments also means having a proper place to display the wares of success. Walk into most any high school and you will find the trophy case for the sports teams. Does your school have a trophy case designated for AECAs? This might not just include the ones from this book, but other common AECAs like band or theatre. I was pleasantly surprised when I was visited Solon City Schools in Ohio. Solon is known for its Science Olympiad teams, which have 12 National Championships between their middle and high school teams, as well as for hosting the Future Problem Solvers State Bowl. I was walking through the cafeteria and was met with trophies in cases (see Figure 6). Many of the AECAs were not only put on display, but also provided with their own trophy case and banner.

Other schools I have visited have displays like Figure 7. Not only were all of the sports activities represented in the displays, but also so were many AECAs, such as debate, Key Club, student council, and Destination Imagination. This is a perfect example of how sports and AECAs can share the stage together and those who normally do not get recognized receive credit for a job well done.

Lastly, honoring your students' accomplishments means having pride in your team. No one would question football players wearing their jerseys to school or baseball players wearing a hat sporting the team's logo. At a lot of the AECA competitions I have attended, teams have made their own T-shirts with the school's name as well as the team name proudly on display. Students should be encouraged to make these shirts as well as wear them to school.

FIGURE 6
Sample Academic Trophy Displays

FIGURE 7
Sample AECA Display

Epilogue

*Enrichment Does Not Just Mean
During the School Day*

A lot of districts make decisions in their gifted departments based on the service they are going to get credit for. In many states, the definition of gifted services only extends to services that take place during the school day. This can mean that, if you provide enrichment to students before school, after school, or on a weekend, it is not considered to be enrichment. Of course we, as educators, know this is baloney. Some of the most powerful learning experiences and enrichment happens to students when they are not sitting at a desk within the concrete walls of a classroom during the hours of normal operation. Many of the most impactful learning moments come when kids are not in school, whether those moments be during an amazing program on astronomy that makes students want to learn more about our universe, or when a student gets a chance to talk to a dentist when they go in to get their teeth cleaned and become fascinated with dental health, or when a student's parents takes them to see a performance of *Hamilton* that causes them to extensively research the Founding Fathers. There are enrichment opportunities all around us every day—called life. We experience things, we learn from them, and then we move forward, taking these new passions or skills with us. Who are we to say that enrichment only happens in the classroom?

Which of these situations do you think would be more powerful—spending a year sitting in a Spanish class learning basic phrases and conjugation, or traveling to Costa Rica during the summer and building sustainable housing immersed in the culture? Or what about learning about democracy in social studies class by reading it in a book versus students volunteering to help campaign for an issue they feel very strongly about? Enrichment can happen in all shapes and sizes, time and places, as well as situations. How can I tell these AECAs are enrichment? Because if you ask a student what they remember about school, they will not talk of an assessment they took, or a book they read, or an assignment they worked on, or a worksheet they completed. The student will remember their involvement in AECAs and what those activities provided. How do I know this? Because that student is my daughter, who participated in Model United Nations, Destination Imagination, Youth and Government, Business Professionals of America, as well as National Honor Society, Safe and Drug Free Schools, and band. These are the activities she talked about when I asked her how her day was. These were the activities that allowed her to present at our Statehouse, travel to Dallas and Anaheim, address more than 1,500 peers with a speech on empowerment, forge lifelong friendships, and create indelible memories. The skills that she learned while participating in these activities, not her ACT score, made her transition to college that much easier. This is why I believe that being able to provide as many of these opportunities for enrichment as possible should be one of the main focuses of the school.

I run AECAs in all 14 buildings in my district. Some of these are before school, others are after, and a few are during the school day. I do everything from homegrown clubs—such as STEM Club, Chess Club, Game Board Club, and Eco Club—to nationally recognized programs—such as Destination Imagination, Invention League, Youth and Government, Model United Nations, and Future City Competition. These clubs are not exclusive to gifted students. For most, anyone in the school can sign up. And yet year after year, I am always surprised at how many gifted children just gravitate toward them. Why is that? Why do gifted students without any provocation on my part, make up a majority of the students participating in these activities? I believe it is because these children are craving enrichment—either enrichment that their school does not offer in the regular day-to-day classroom or enrichment that looks very different from what they experience in their classes. These are authentic experiences where their academic skills and abilities get to shine.

What are we, as educators, going to do in our own districts to turn the focus to such activities? What can we do to support enrichment activities, provide resources, and make them available to all students who want to participate? These AECAs need advocates such as yourself in order to be successful. The question I am going to end with is this: What's your next step?

References

America's Battle of the Books. (n.d.). https://www.battleofthebooks.org

Berkowitz, S. (2018, March 7). *NCAA reports revenues of more than $1 billion in 2017*. USA Today. https://www.usatoday.com/story/sports/college/2018/03/07/ncaa-reports-revenues-more-than-1-billion-2017/402486002

Black, R. (2019, September 12). *Glossophobia (fear of public speaking): Are you glossophobic?* Psycom. https://www.psycom.net/glossophobia-fear-of-public-speaking

Blauvelt, D. O., & Cote, R. G. (2012). *Order in the court: A mock trial simulation: An interactive discovery-based social studies unit for high-ability learners*. Prufrock Press.

Business Professionals of America. (n.d.-a). *Competitive event listing*. https://bpa.org/students/compete/competitive-event-listing

Business Professionals of America. (n.d.-b). *Educators: Start here*. https://bpa.org/educators

Cherry, K. (2019). *Overview of emotional intelligence.* VeryWell Mind. https://www.verywellmind.com/what-is-emotional-intelligence-2795423

DECA. (n.d.). *Competitive events.* https://www.deca.org/high-school-programs/high-school-competitive-events

DECA. (2019). *This is how we do DECA: The ultimate advisor guidebook.* https://www.deca.org/wp-content/uploads/2019/09/2019_Advisor_Guidebook.pdf

Destination Imagination. (n.d.). *2020–21 challenge previews.* https://www.destinationimagination.org/challenge-program/2020-21-challenge-previews

FIRST LEGO League. (n.d.). *Impact.* https://www.firstinspires.org/robotics/fll/impact

Future City Competition. (n.d.-a). *2017–18 challenge: The age-friendly city.* https://futurecity.org/region/2017-18-challenge

Future City Competition. (n.d.-b). *Competition deliverables.* https://futurecity.org/about-the-competition/competition-deliverables

Future City Competition. (n.d.-c). *Leading your team.* https://futurecity.org/leading-your-team

Future City Competition. (n.d.-d). *Our impact.* https://futurecity.org/page/our-impact

Future City Competition. (n.d.-e). *Welcome to Houston Texas Future City regional competition 2019–2020.* https://futurecity.org/texas-houston

Future Problem Solving Program International. (n.d.-a). *21st century learning skills.* https://www.fpspi.org/21st-century-learning-skills

Future Problem Solving Program International. (n.d.-b). *Competitive components.* https://www.fpspi.org/competitive-components

Future Problem Solving Program International. (2020, June 16). In *Wikipedia.* https://en.wikipedia.org/wiki/Future_Problem_Solving_Program_International

Goetz, K. (2011, February 1). *How 3M gave everyone days off and created an innovation dynamo.* Fast Company. https://www.fastcompany.com/1663137/how-3m-gave-everyone-days-off-and-created-an-innovation-dynamo

Illinois Science Olympiad. (n.d.). *Regional tournaments.* https://www.illinoisolympiad.org/regionals.html

Invention Convention. (n.d.). https://inventionconvention.org/home-page

Lynch, M. (2019, January 12). *7 benefits of STEM education.* The EdVocate. https://www.theedadvocate.org/7-benefits-of-stem-education

Kiwanis International. (n.d.). *Key Club advisor guide.* https://s3.amazonaws.com/keyclub-wpassets/wp-content/uploads/2017/08/24130804/Guide_Faculty_Kiwanis-Advisor-Guide.pdf

MATHCOUNTS. (n.d.-a). *MATHCOUNTS competition series.* https://www.mathcounts.org/programs/competition-series

MATHCOUNTS. (n.d.-b). *MATHCOUNTS practice plans.* https://www.math counts.org/mathcounts-practice-plans

MATHCOUNTS. (2019). *Problem of the week archive. In with the new—December 23, 2019.* https://www.mathcounts.org/sites/default/files/images/potw/pdf/PoTW122319%20Solutions.pdf

NACLO. (n.d.-a). *Information for students.* http://www.naclo.cs.cmu.edu/stu dentFAQ.html

NACLO. (n.d.-b). *Magicsquare.* https://www.nacloweb.org/resources/problems/sample/Magicsquare.pdf

National Association for Gifted Children. (n.d.). *Leadership.* https://www.nagc.org/resources-publications/resources/social-emotional-issues/leadership

National Geographic. (n.d.). *GeoBeeFAQs.* https://www.nationalgeographic.org/education/student-experiences/geobee/faq

National High School Mock Trial Championship. (2020). *Rules of the competition.* https://www.nationalmocktrial.org/rules/rules-competition

National Speech and Debate Association. (n.d.-a). *Competition events.* https://www.speechanddebate.org/competition-events

National Speech and Debate Association. (n.d.-b). *Explore membership.* https://www.speechanddebate.org/explore-membership-students

Rube Goldberg. (n.d.-a). *Contests.* https://www.rubegoldberg.com/contests-landing

Rube Goldberg. (n.d.-b). *Past tasks.* https://www.rubegoldberg.com/contests/history/past-tasks

Scholastic Art & Writing Awards. (n.d.-a). *The alliance.* https://www.artand writing.org/the-alliance

Scholastic Art & Writing Awards. (n.d.-b). *How to enter.* https://www.artand writing.org/awards/how-to-enter

Science Olympiad. (n.d.). *Start a team.* https://www.soinc.org/join/start-team

Society for Industrial and Applied Mathematics. (n.d.). *The challenge.* MathWorks Math Modeling Challenge. https://m3challenge.siam.org/challenge

Society for Industrial and Applied Mathematics. (2018). *Scoring guidelines.* MathWorks Math Modeling Challenge. https://m3challenge.siam.org/sites/default/files/uploads/M3%20Challenge_Scoring%20Guide_generic.pdf

Stanley, T. (2018). *Authentic learning: Real-world experiences that build 21st-century skills.* Prufrock Press.

Veliz, P., Snyder, M., & Sabo, D. (2019). *The state of high school sports in America: An evaluation of the nation's most popular extracurricular activity.* Women's Sports Foundation.

Wagner, T. (2014). *The global achievement gap: Why even our best schools don't teach the new survival skills our children need—and what we can do about it* (Rev. ed.). Basic Books.

Wai, J., & Allen, J. (2019). What boosts talent development? Examining predictors of academic growth in secondary school among academically advanced youth across 21 years. *Gifted Children Quarterly, 63*(4), 253–272. https://doi.org/10.1177/0016986219869042

WordMasters Challenge. (n.d.). *Using analogies to master vocabulary.* https://www.wordmasterschallenge.com

WordMasters Challenge. (2020). *WordMasters Challenge schedule.* https://www.wordmasterschallenge.com/challenge-schedule

World Economic Forum. (2018). *The future of jobs report 2018.* http://www3.weforum.org/docs/WEF_Future_of_Jobs_2018.pdf

About the Author

Todd Stanley is the author of many teacher education books, including *Project-Based Learning for Gifted Students: A Step-by-Step Guide to PBL and Inquiry in the Classroom* (2nd ed.), *Authentic Learning: Real-World Experiences That Build 21st-Century Skills*, and *Using Rubrics for Performance-Based Assessment: A Practical Guide to Evaluating Student Work*. He was a classroom teacher for 18 years, teaching students as young as second graders and as old as high school seniors, and was a National Board Certified teacher. He is currently gifted services coordinator for Pickerington Local School District, OH, where he lives with his wife, Nicki, and two daughters, Anna and Abby. You can follow Todd on Twitter @the_gifted_guy, or you can visit his website at https://www.thegiftedguy.com, where there are many free resources available, including blogs, professional development video tutorials, and classroom materials.

For Product Safety Concerns and Information please contact our EU
representative GPSR@taylorandfrancis.com Taylor & Francis Verlag GmbH,
Kaufingerstraße 24, 80331 München, Germany

Printed and bound by CPI Group (UK) Ltd, Croydon, CR0 4YY

08/06/2025
01896981-0005